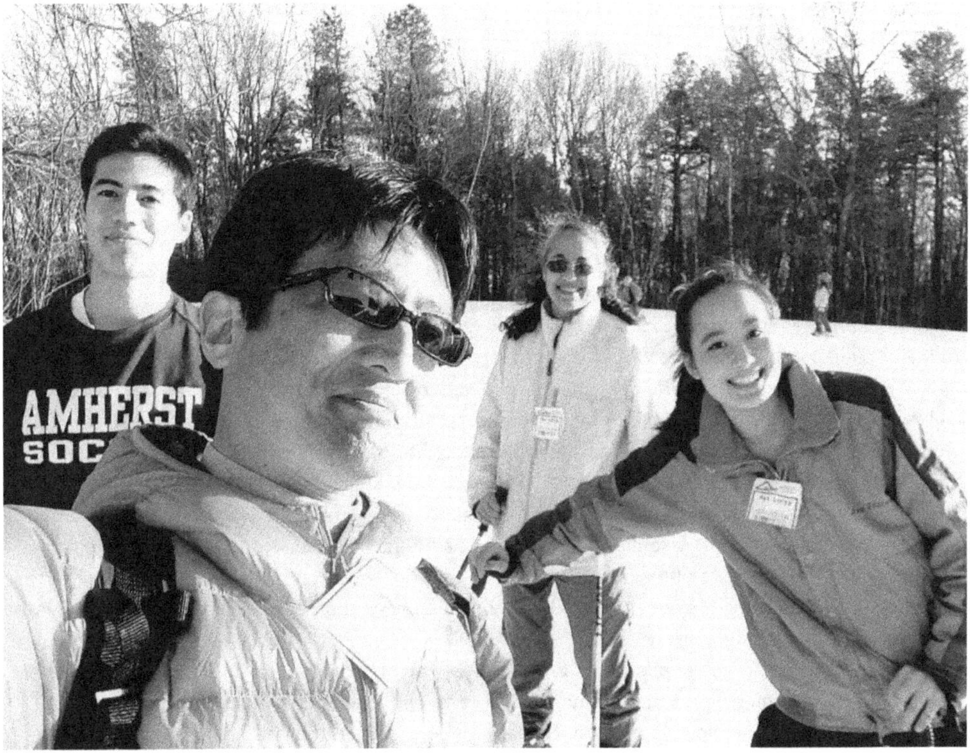

The Freedom to Dream

2020

Prologue: Double 2~The Freedom to Dream, 2020~

Double2 The Freedom to Dream is the electronic and updated version of *Double* which was originally published in 2005 and *Double2* originally electronically published in 2013. To make it easy to follow, the content of the previous two books are included in this edition. The voice of Double and, in fact, his whole family have changed greatly in the intervening years.
Additionally, this edition provides updates on the thoughts of Double and the family's life during the reunion of the family in 2020 due to the COVID-19 pandemic.
What exactly has changed in the past 25 years? What has remained the same? Why? Meditating on those questions while re-examining our photos has led me to the words on these pages.
Children grow up. This gives us adults a chance to grow as well. Have we made something of that chance or not? There are many regrets. Have there also been moments of pride? Updating this book has had me thinking acutely about these issues.
When the original book was published in 2005, those who supported it most enthusiastically were female junior and senior high school students. They are now all adults. I am sure they are not just "fine" but unique and special women. Some may be mothers of a child with their own "I" voice. I am fascinated to know how *Double2 The Freedom to Dream 2020* appears to them now.

Kazuhiko Iimura, June 2020

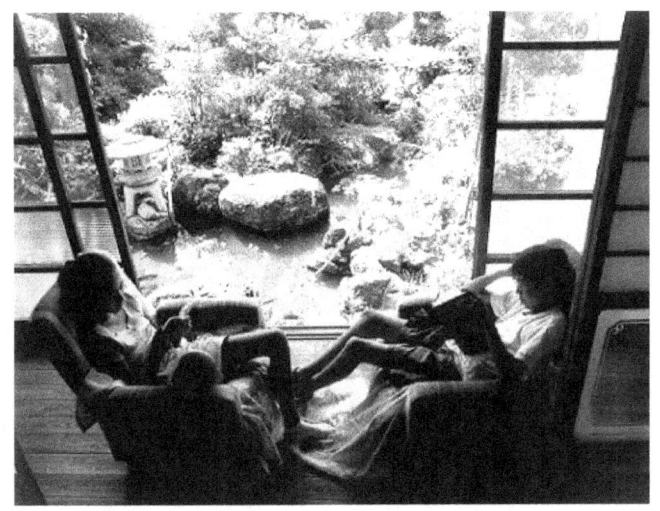

double^2

Kazuhiko Iimura

Translator: Brett Iimura

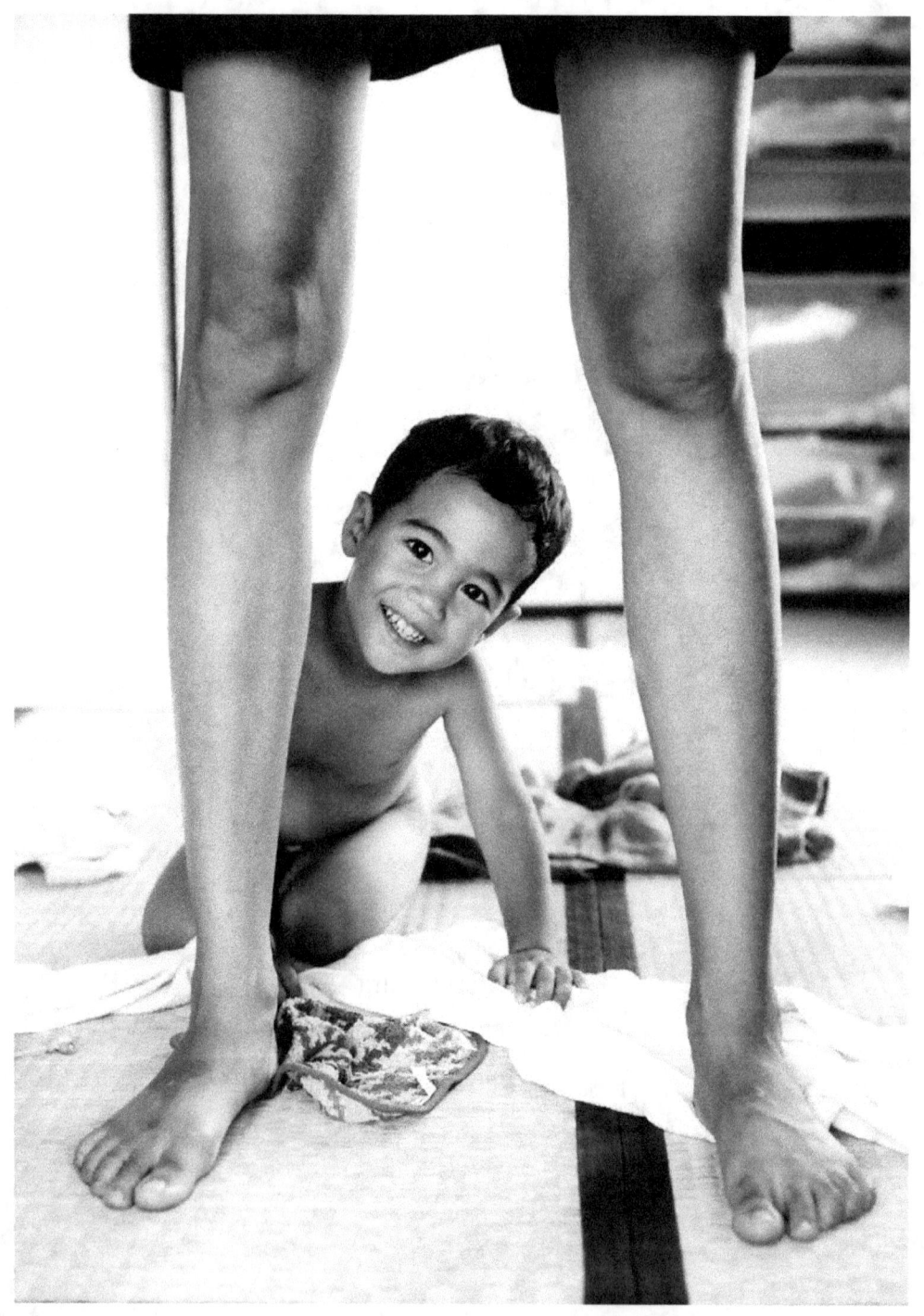

Double

My Daddy is Japanese.
My Mommy is American.
I am both Japanese and American.
So,
In other words,
I am neither.

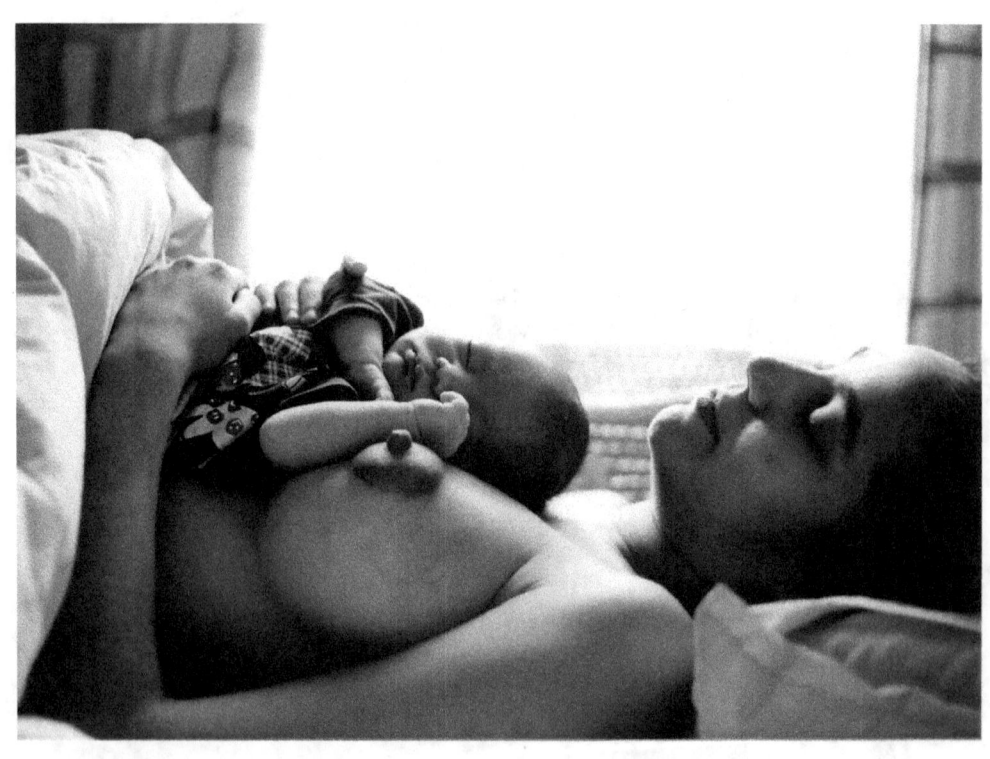

<u>Cocoon</u>

You ask me, how does it feel to be born?
Well,
Gravity is overwhelmingly powerful,
Air feels heavy and oppressive.
So,
It's rather hard to breathe.
Actually,
It's quite tough.

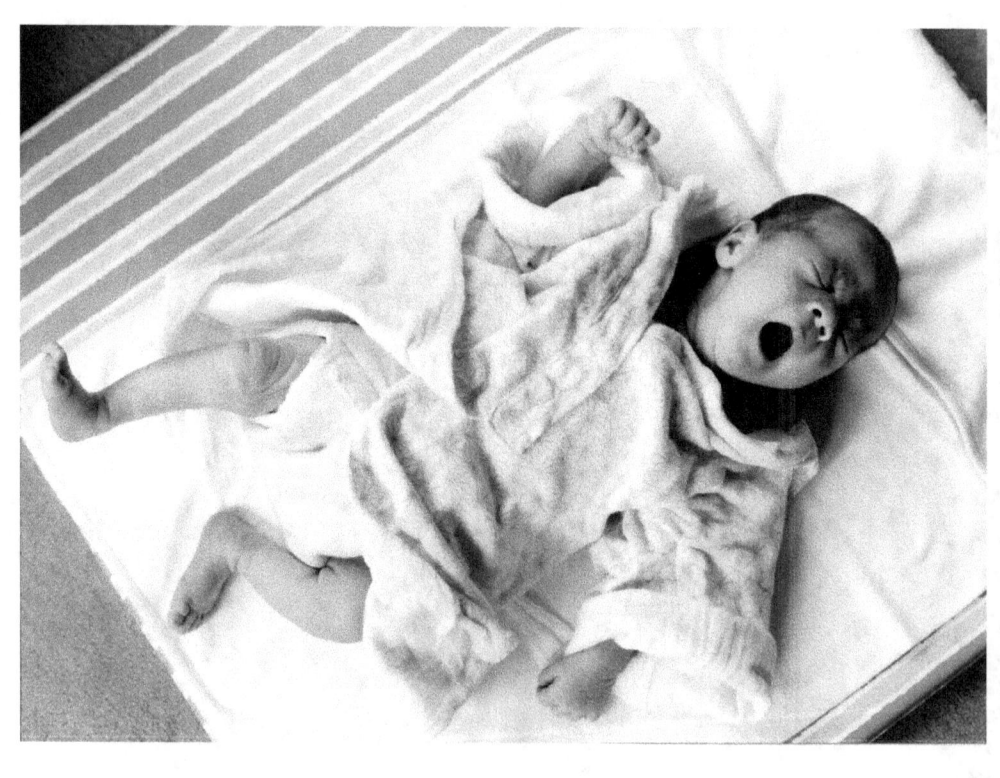

A Sound Spirit

My body is made up of carbon and hydrogen and oxygen.
But,
Having only that is kind of dull,
don't you think?
So,
I also have emotions
That blew into me
While I was in my Mommy's womb.

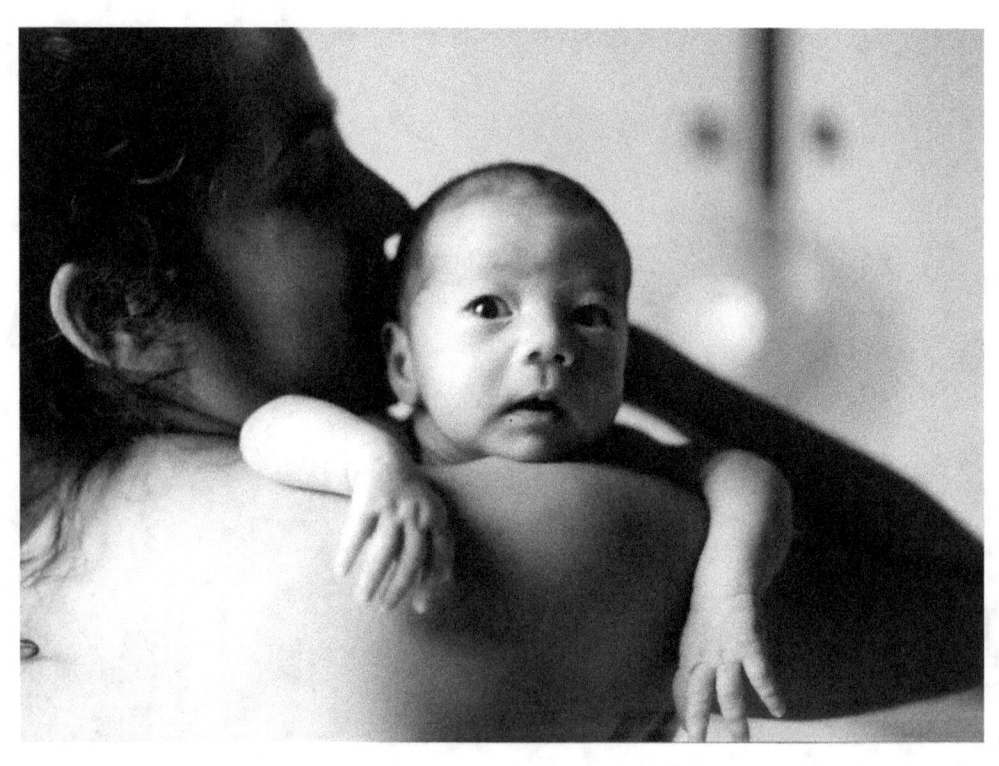

A frog? I suppose...

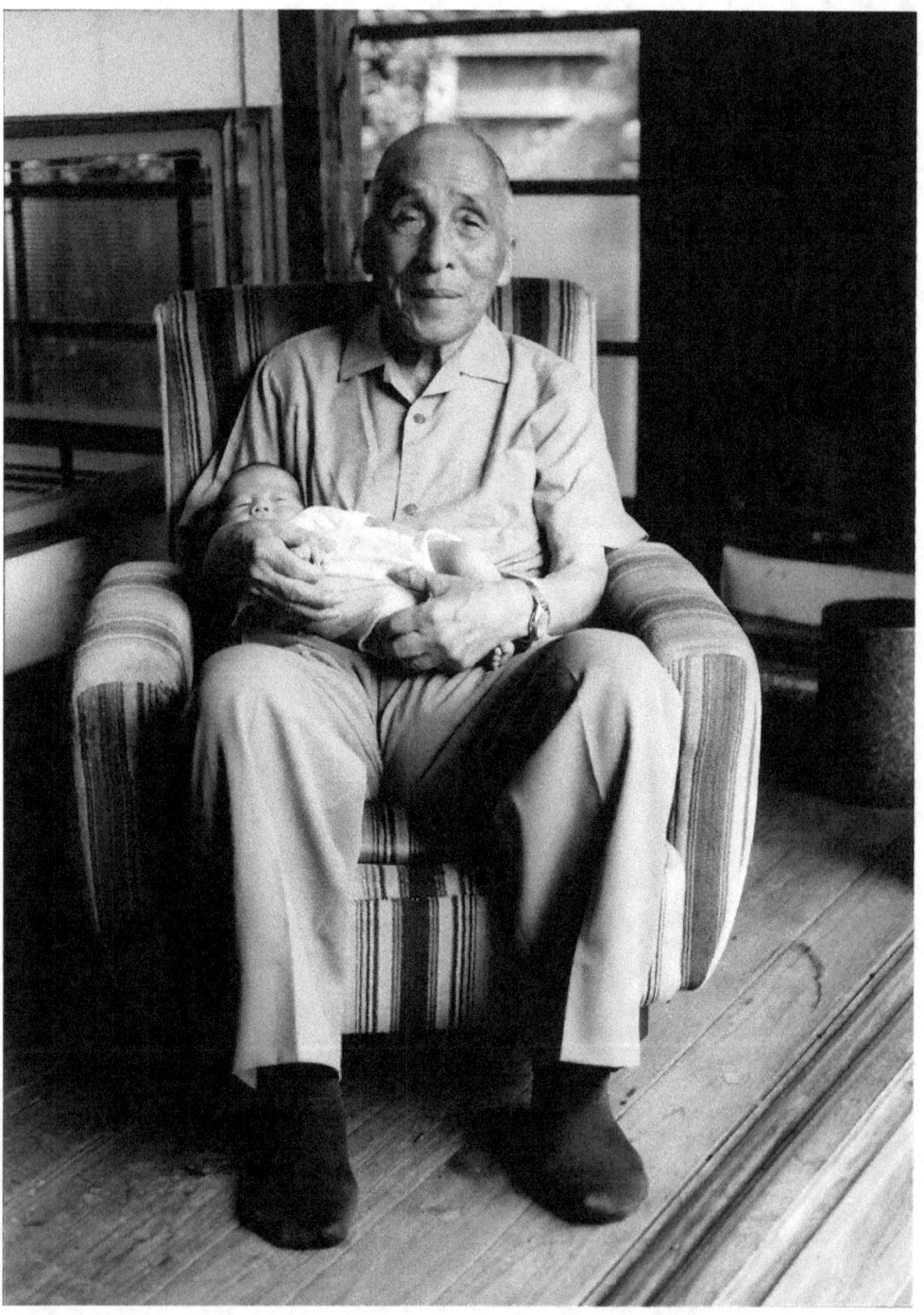

The Deepest Valley

My Great-Grandfather murmured,
"Noa's head is a good shape."
In order to jump over the deepest valley,
Hope is needed.

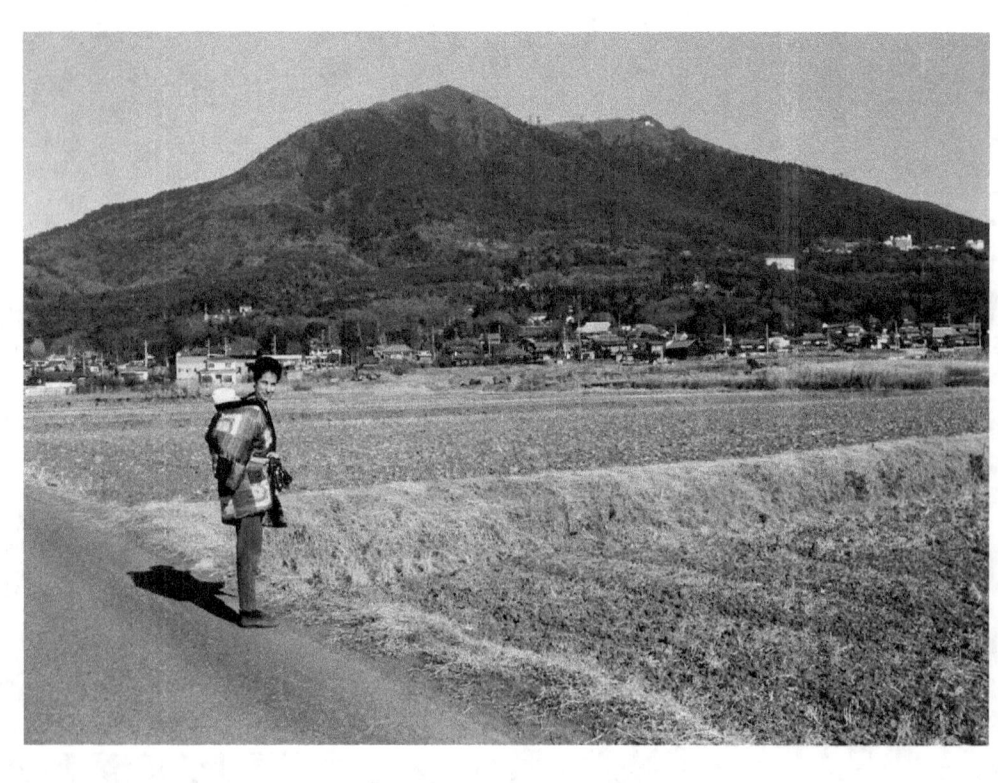

The Mountain Speaks Intimately

"It's fine to be strange,
To be different."
My Mommy says that all the time.
If that's so,
Then you can follow your dreams
Forever.

A Greek Man

When my Daddy lived in NY,
He would go every morning for coffee
At the Greek diner.
He always went.
Nothing more than that.
But the Greek waiter gave me a $20 bill when I was born.
In Greece, it seems,
There is a tradition of "silvering" the baby
By giving them silver coins.
He "silvered" me.

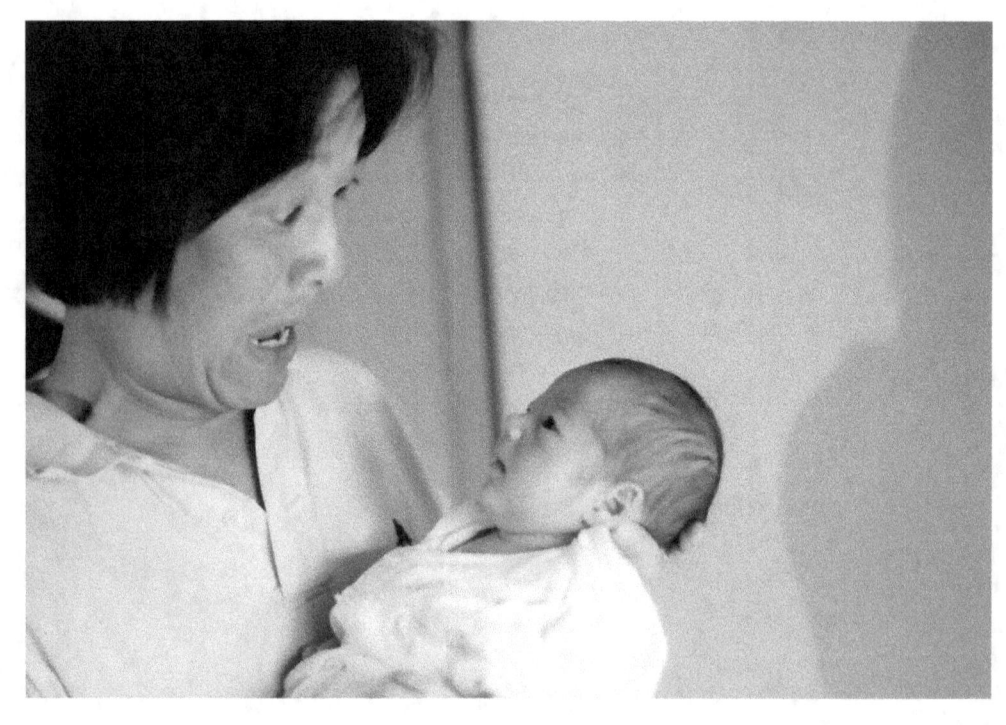

Someone Who Must Be Loved

The first time I met him,
My Uncle Aki's face was just as he is.
Warm and bright,
A truly sensitive person
Who must be loved.
My Uncle Aki will always, always
Look to me as he did then.
My Daddy says,
When someone touches a newborn
They are who they really are.

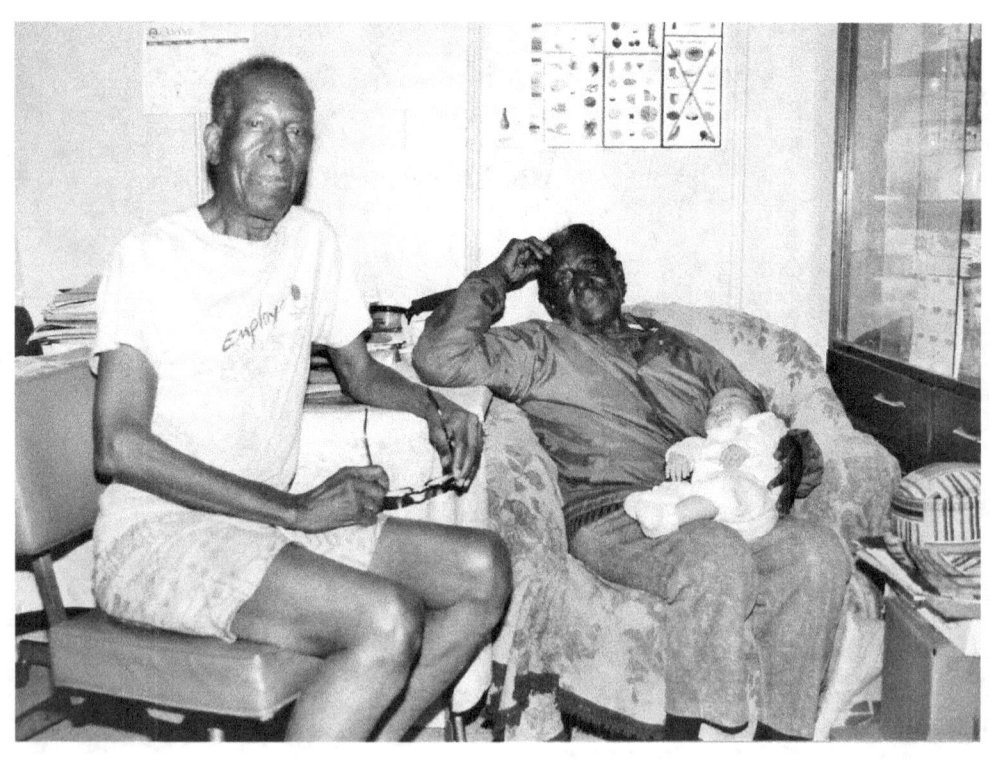

My Mommy's Friends

A beautiful, glossy color.
It makes me look really pale.
They are my Mommy's friends from when she was my age.
"I changed your Mommy's diapers!"
She laughs as she says that.
Her husband nods his head in agreement.
Really?

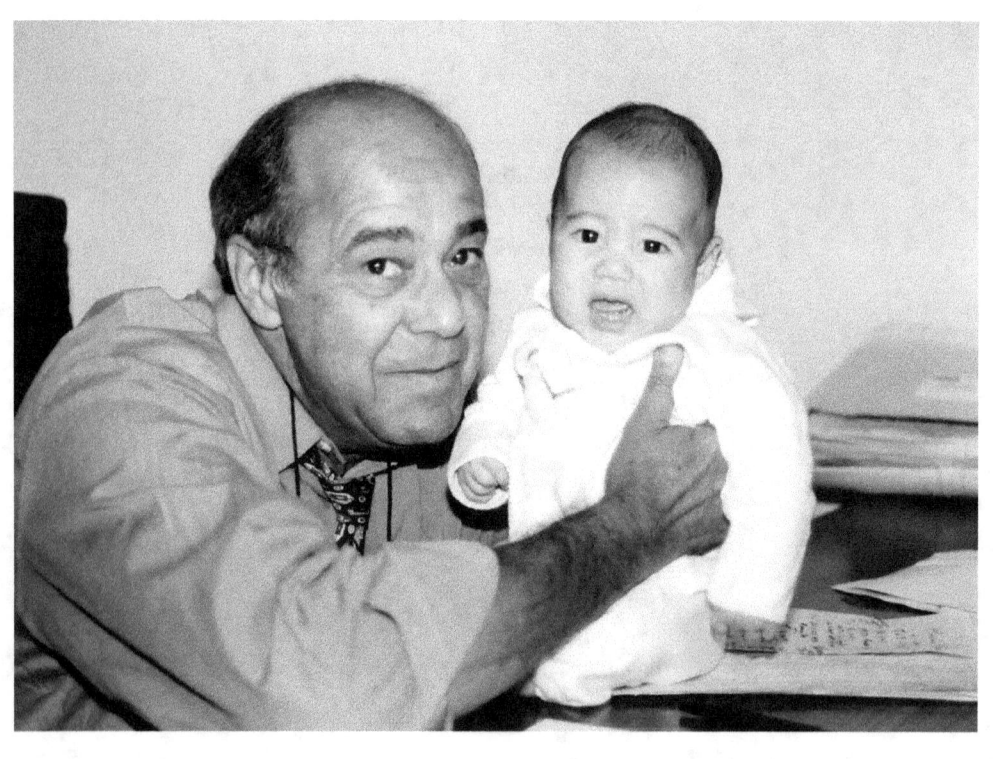

Look-Alikes

Me and him,
It's said we look a lot alike.
Which means that,
When I am the same age as my Mommy's father,
My hair will be just like it is now?

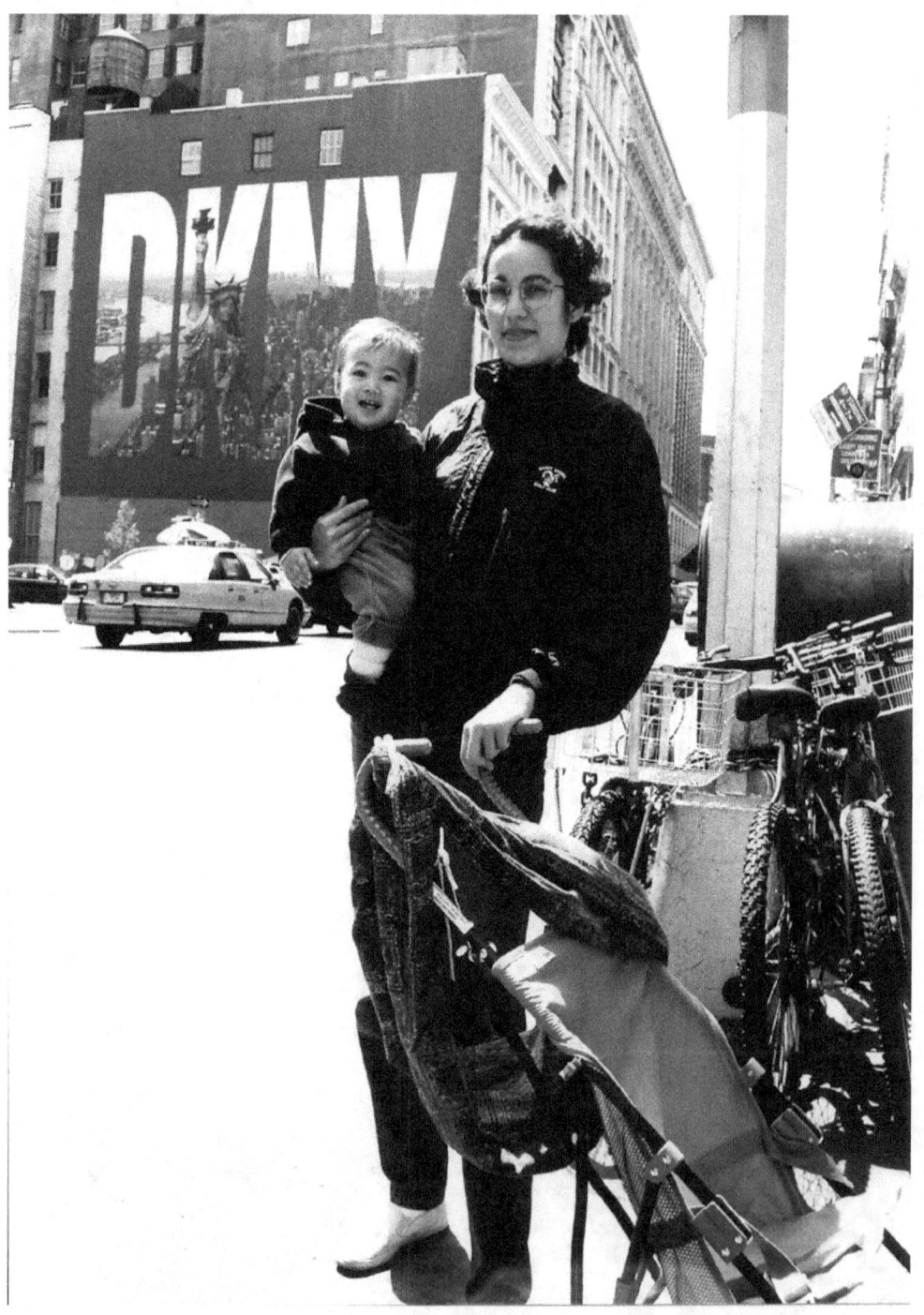

Manhattan

Doesn't my Mommy
Look like Joan of Arc?
Well,
I don't know.
I've never met her.

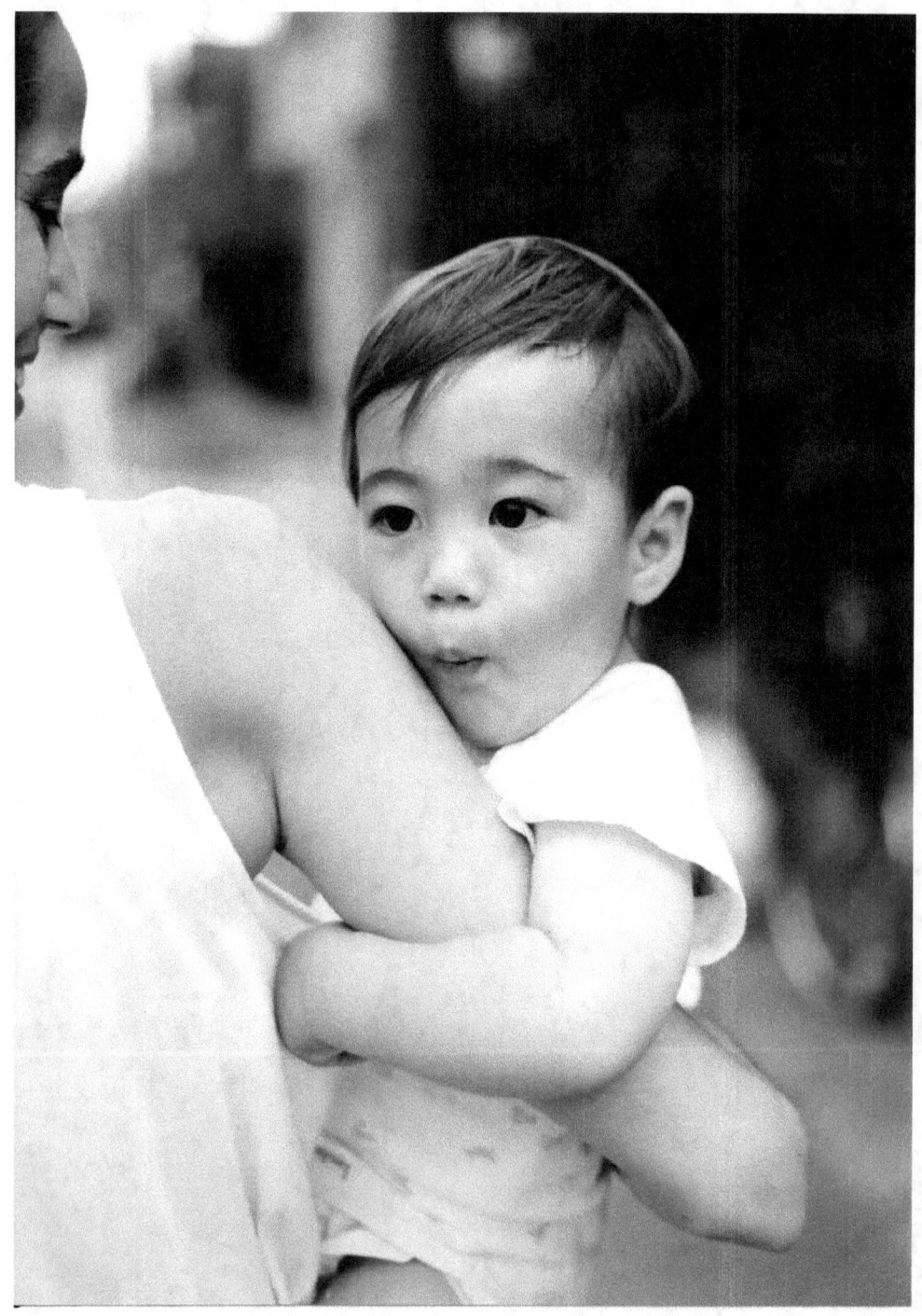

"O" Face

One of my faults is
Whenever I find something interesting,
I can't pull myself away from it.
If things continue like this
Then by the time I'm in junior high
There won't be anything left for me to learn.
But,
I can't stop myself.
Oh!
Another exclamation point!

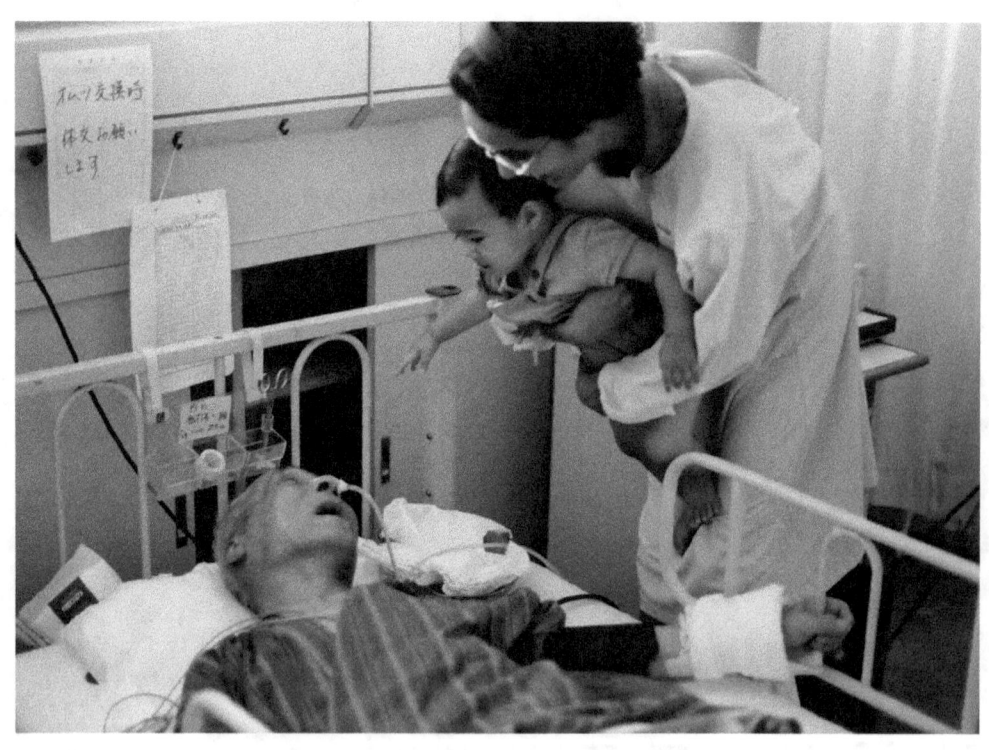

Once Upon A Time

"Hey!" I called.

My Great-Grandfather's lips moved.

He looked up at me.

I thought he was going to hug me as usual…

His hands tried to move toward me

but they couldn't.

That's strange.

But when I looked more closely

I saw my Great-Grandfather's hands tied to the bed.

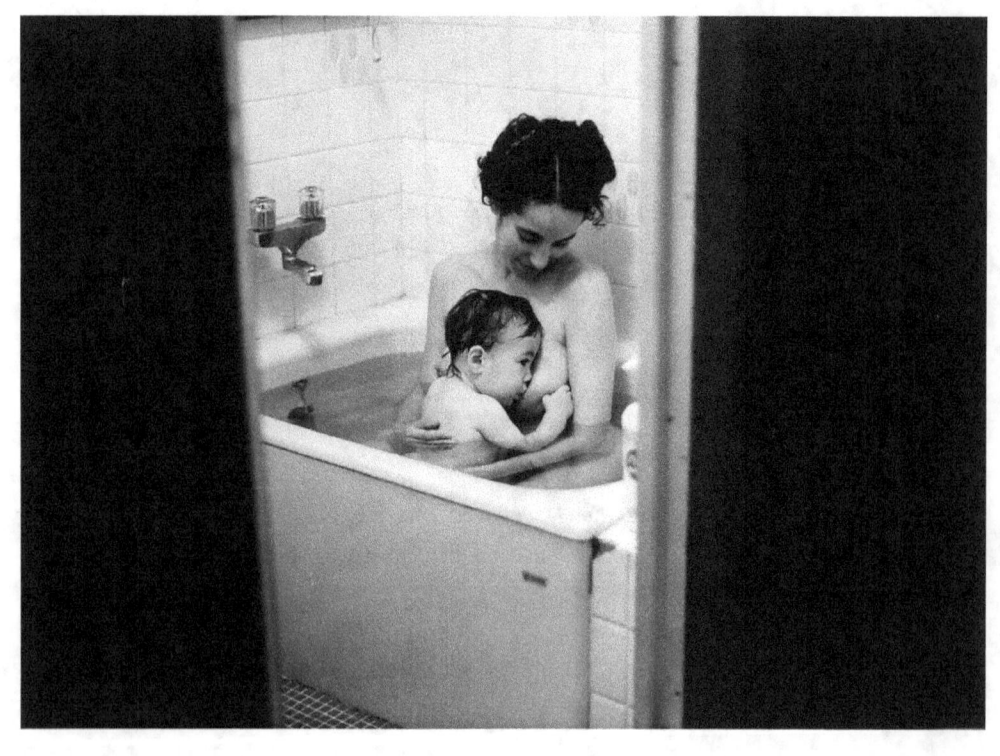

The Meaning of Mum-mums

I know.

Life is short.

Nothing lasts forever.

Even if you leave it alone, it comes around.

So,

More than tomorrow,

The Mum-mums in front of me right now

Are absolutely, positively more important.

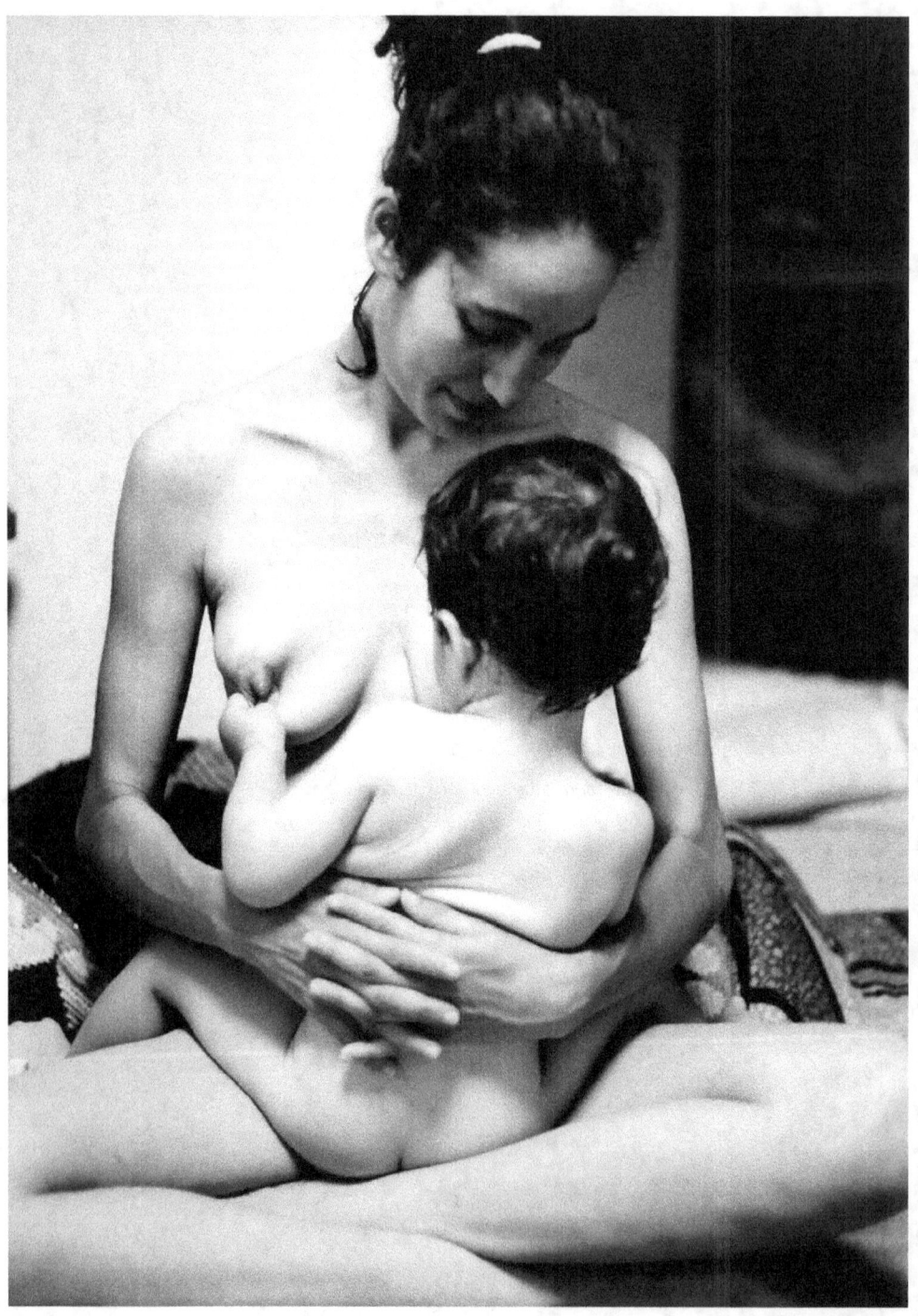

Professional Fingertips

I am an expert on Mum-mums.
I know just where to squeeze
to get the most out.
The way I use my left hand
is exquisite,
isn't it?

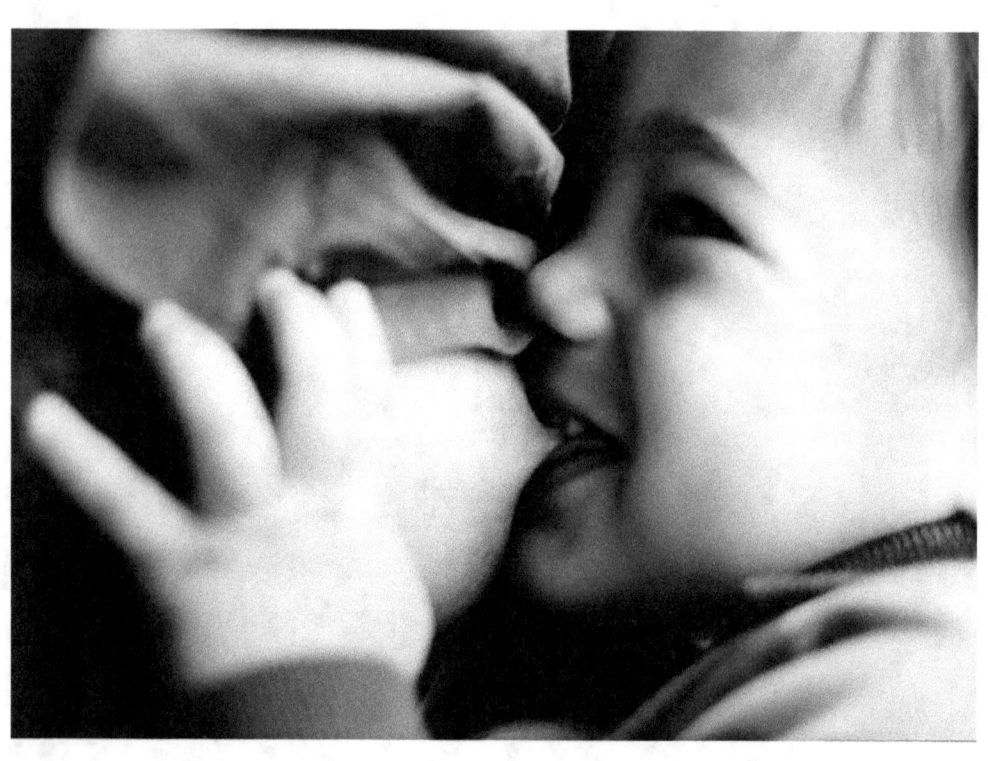

But it's a little embarrassing

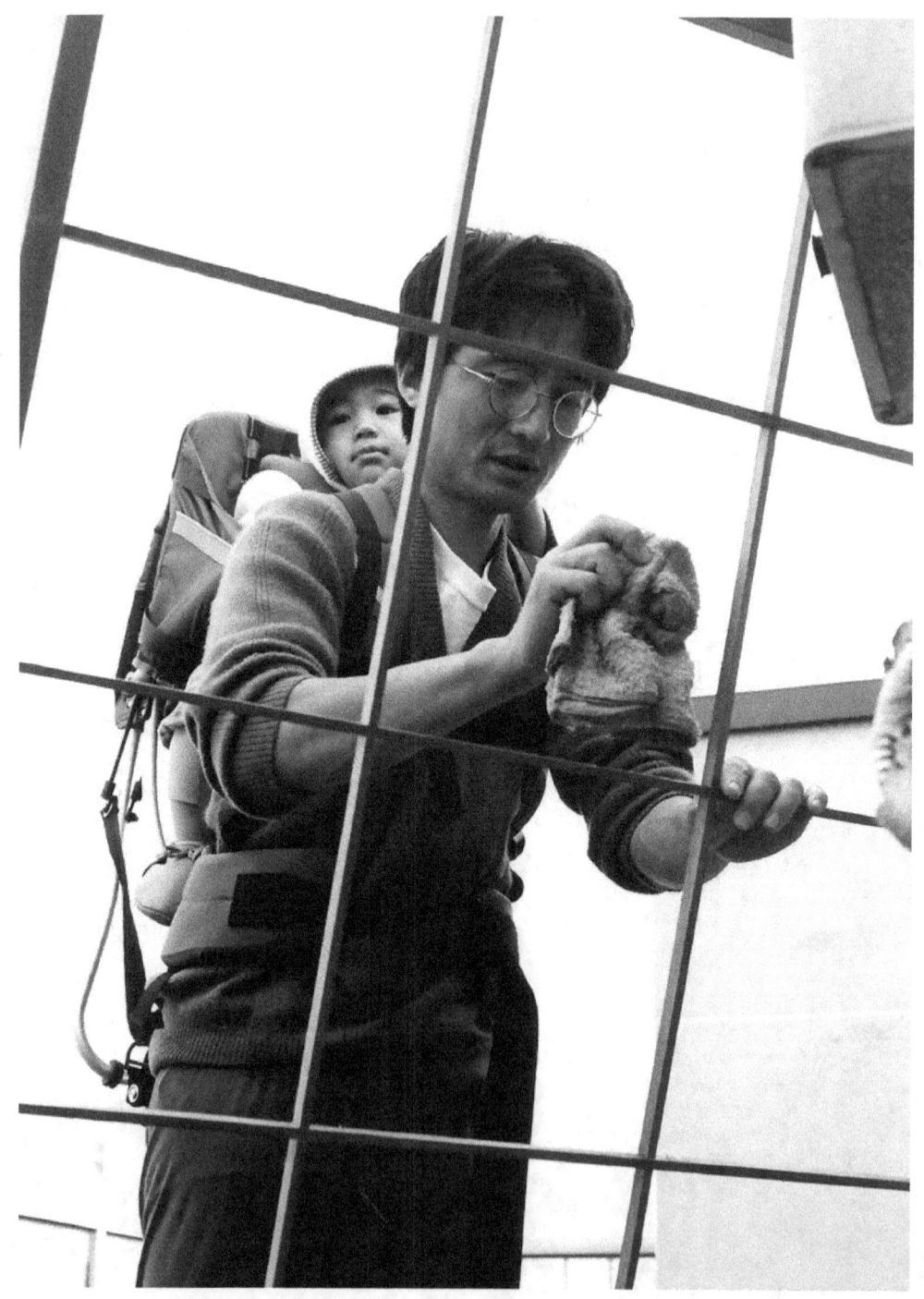

Backs

My Daddy's back
is nice and warm,
but it smells sweaty.
That's what is different
between he and my Mommy.

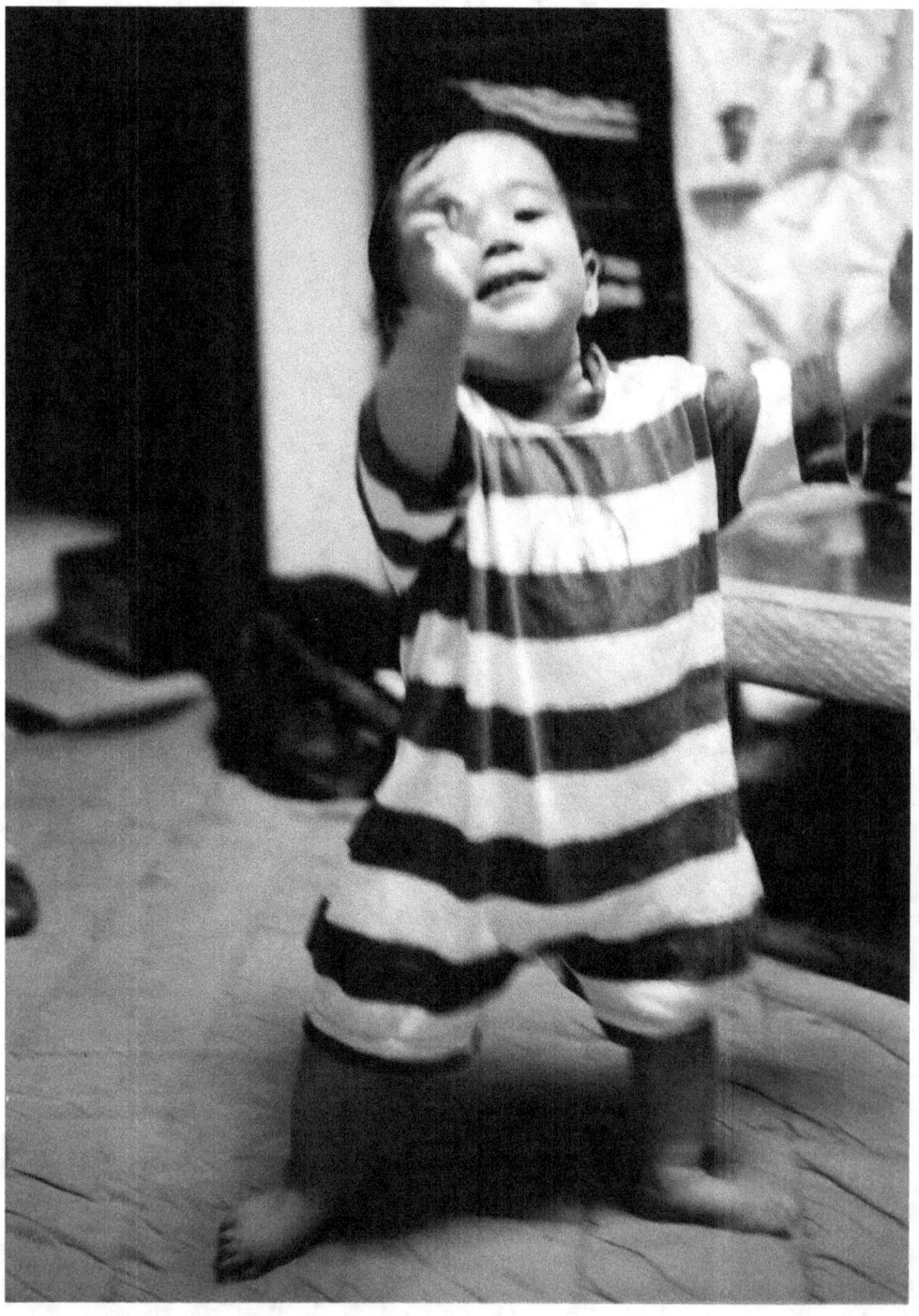

One Great Step…

It's absolutely, positively true.
The pure, unadulterated super shot.
My Mommy took this photo.
Wasn't it Armstrong or someone who said
Something about one step in Hollywood (or was it the moon?)
That was nothing compared with my one step.
Because my one step
Was proof
That I am human.

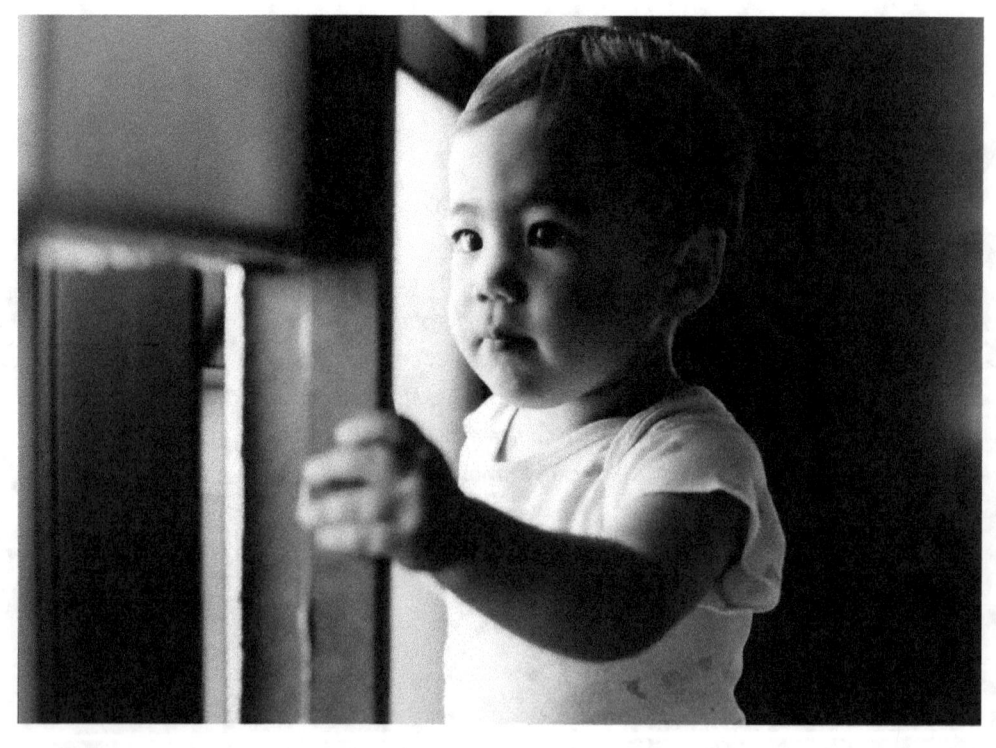

Like /Don't Like

◎ *Concentrating*
× *Repressing emotions, calming down*
× *Being shocked*
× *Inertia*
× *Staying calm*
× *Calculating pragmatism*
○ *Insight*
○ *Responsibility*
× *Boredom*

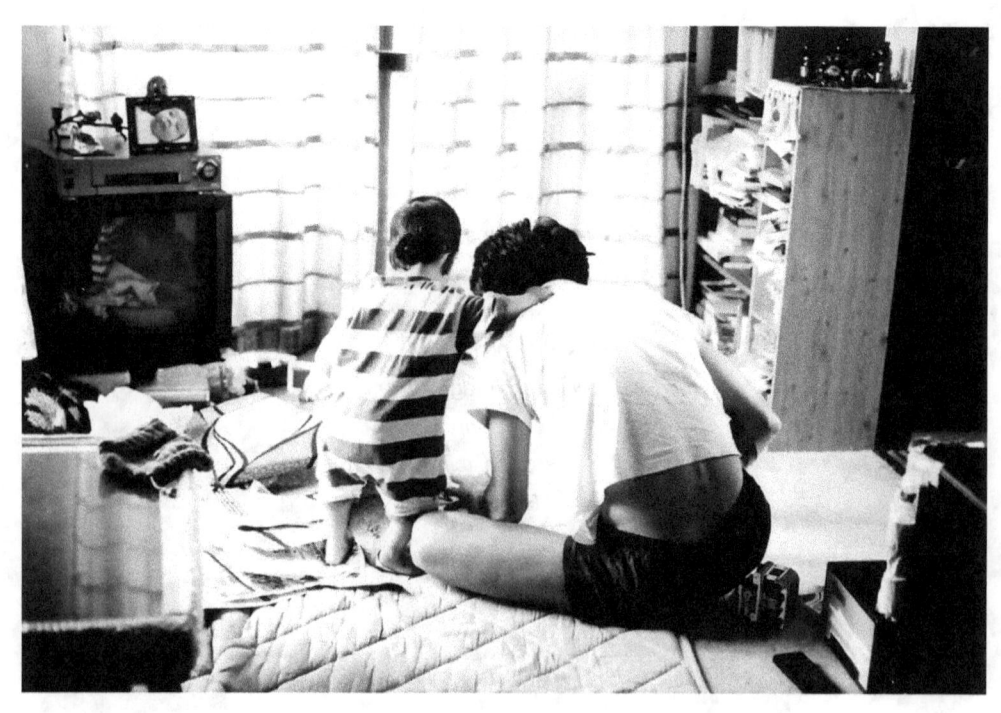

Hey! What's Up?

When my Daddy is depressed
he's not cool.
So, at those times,
I tell him to cheer up
by patting him on the shoulder.
We're both men after all.
That's how we communicate.

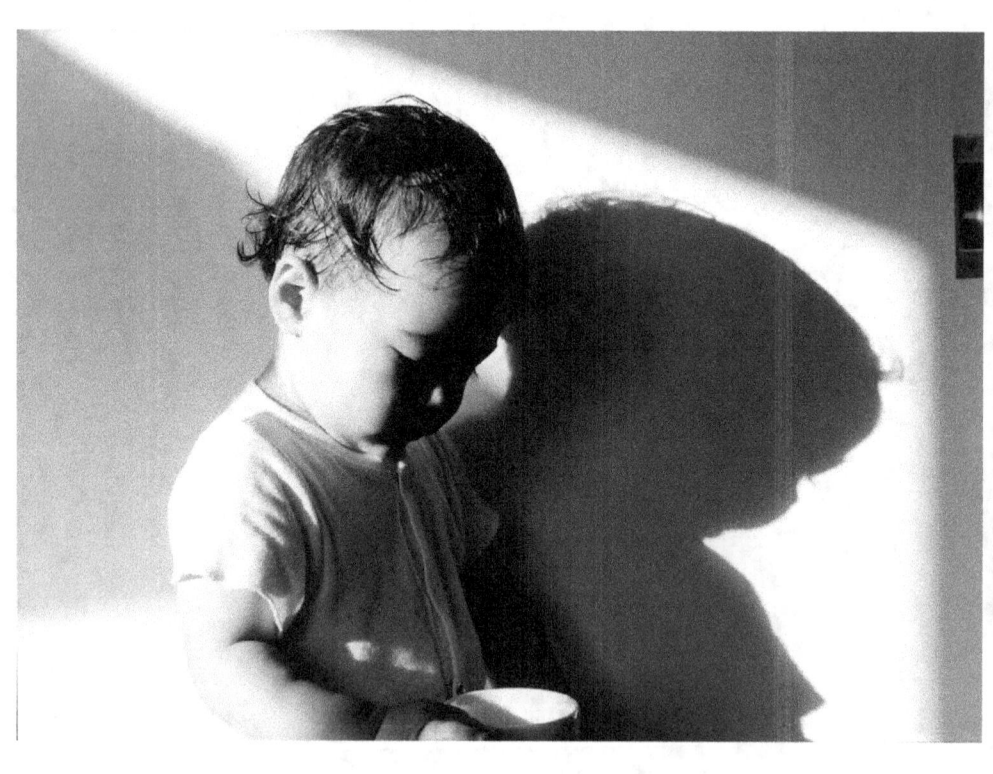

What's "medium"?

For me,
There is no medium.
In my Mommy's language,
You say "so,so."
I never feel "medium,"
Halfway nowhere.
I'm always feeling either terrific or lousy.

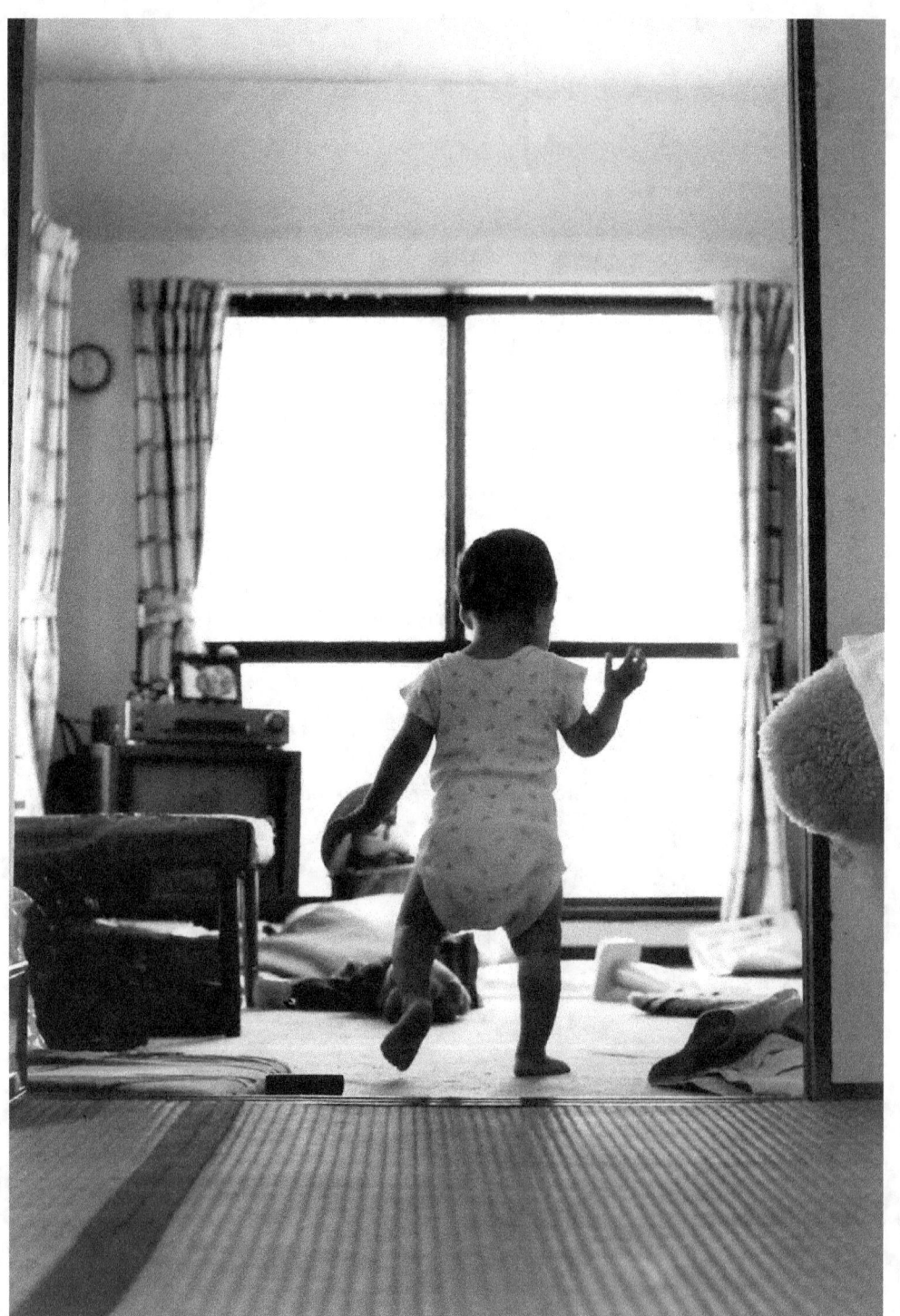

The Slow Goodbye

I will probably just lightly wave my right hand and say,
"See you around,"
when I leave the nest.
Mommy, Daddy,
Please don't cry.
That's how it's supposed to be.

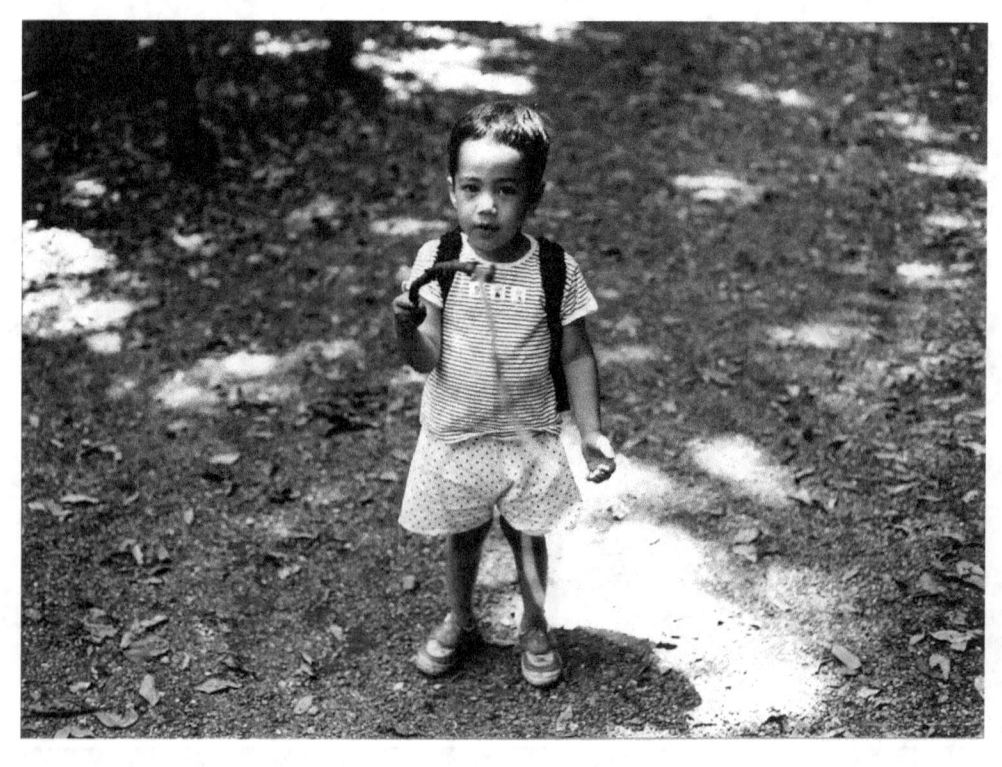

Eye Level

What interests me when I take a walk?
Well,
A flower beginning to bloom.
A dog walking toward me with an inscrutable face.

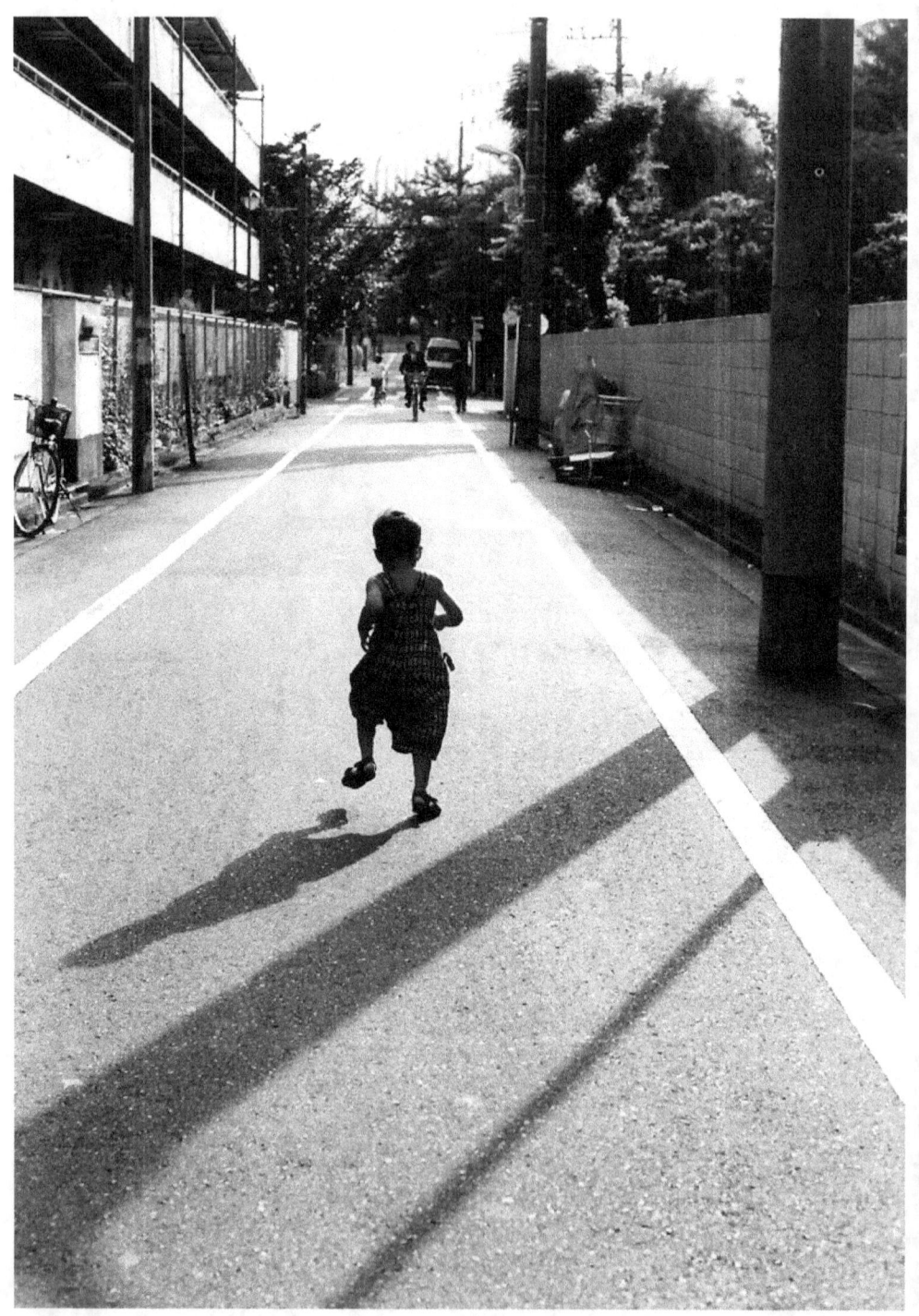

Born to Run

I don't understand the reason why
but sometimes I just feel like running.
My Daddy watches me and says,
"When you put your all into it, Noa,
everyone puts their all into it."
That doesn't make me feel bad.
But when I say,
"Daddy, let's run together!"
he never seems to start running.
I don't know why.

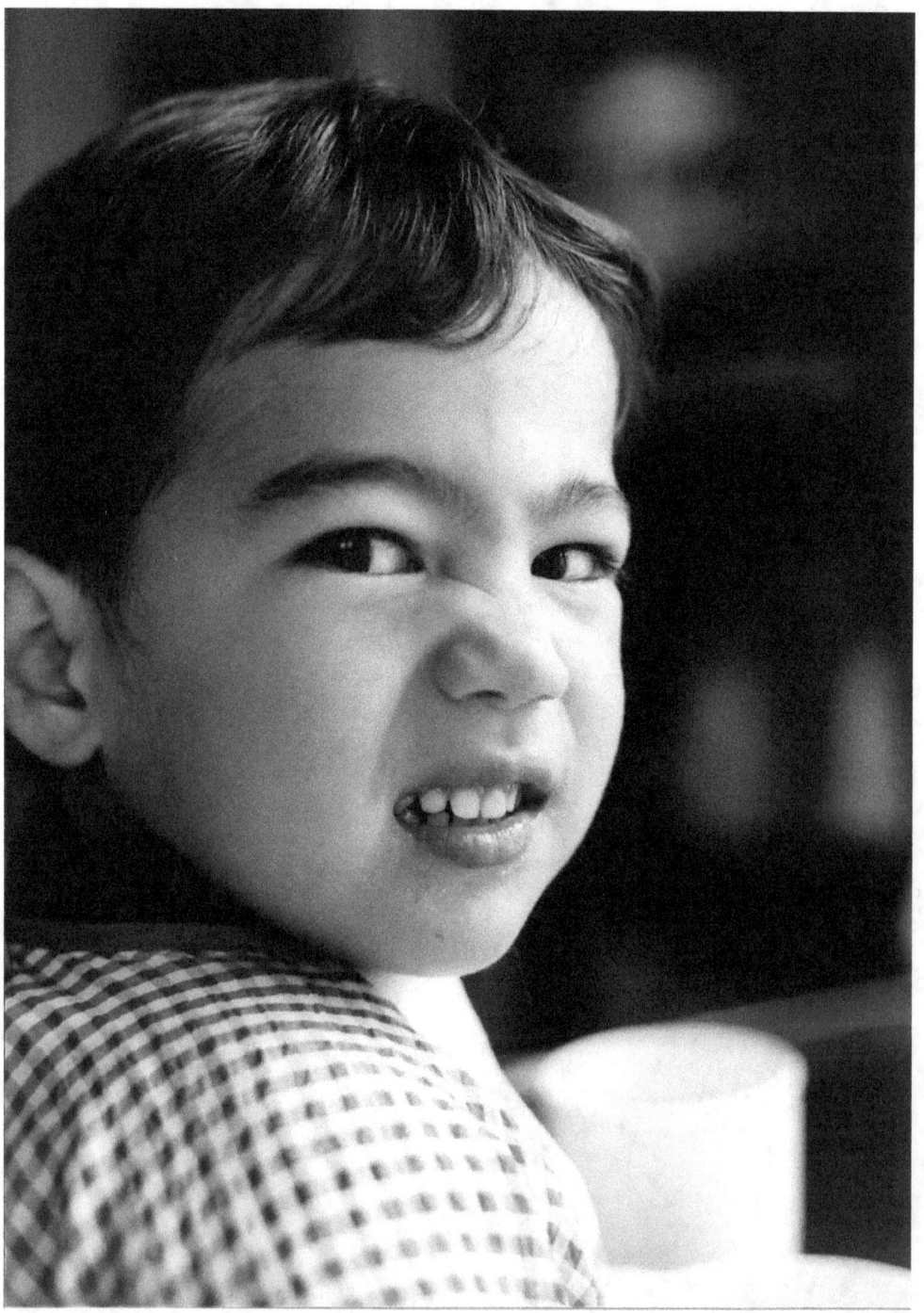

I Won't Break

If a person is too free
it seems they break.
My Daddy told me that one time.
"Most grownups don't have the ability
to make correct choices
by themselves."
I'm safe on that score.
Why do you think?
The answer is because I'm a _____ .

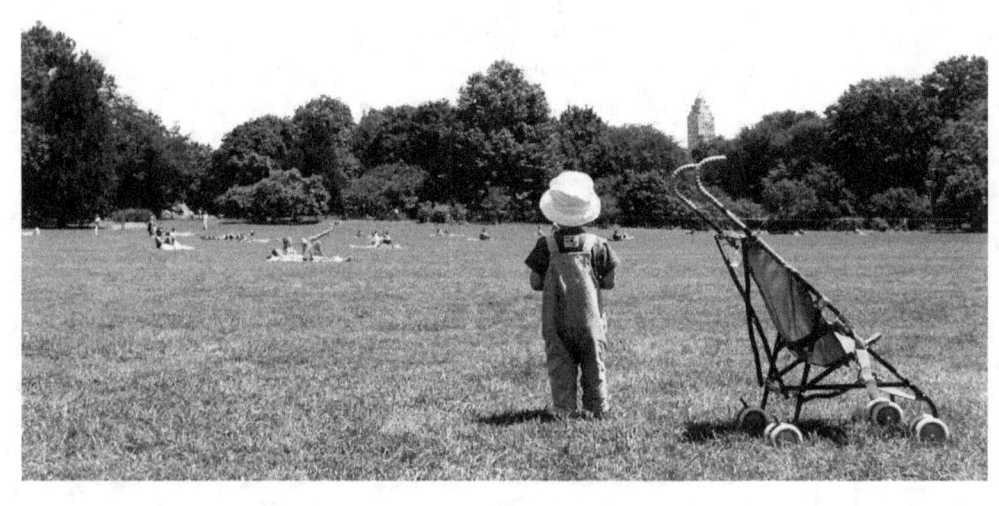

Boredom

When you're not doing anything
What's the thing
that increases along with the passage of time?
Boredom.
Nothing happens.
No pain. No itchiness.
No tension. No excitement.
11am. Bland and dry.
I can't put up with that.

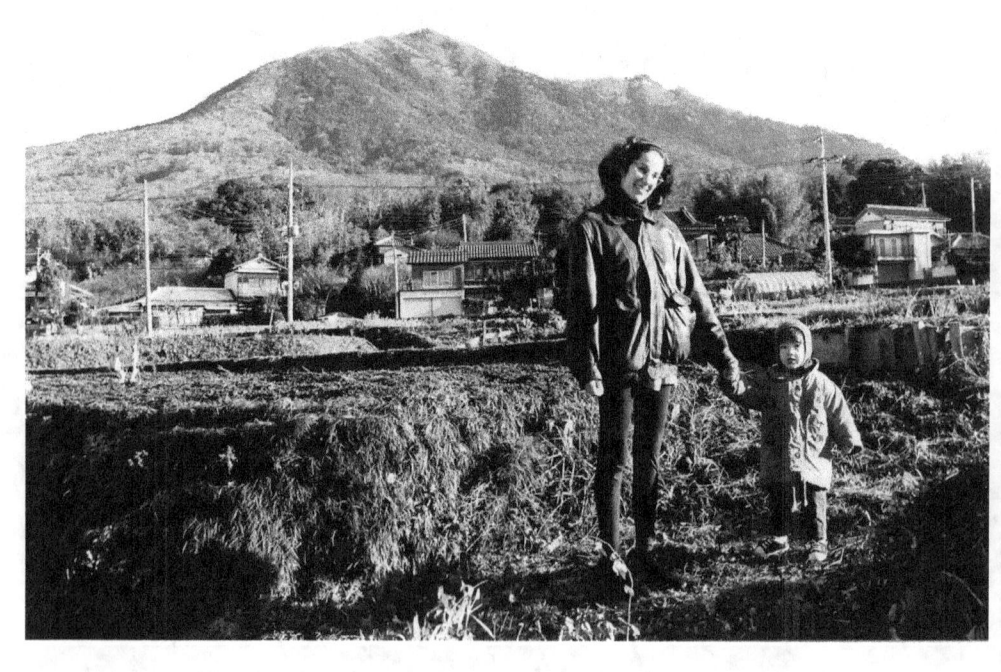

Oh, Give Me a Home…

According to my Mommy,
A person's hometown
Is not the place where you were born.
It's wherever you feel at ease
And can be
Who you really are.

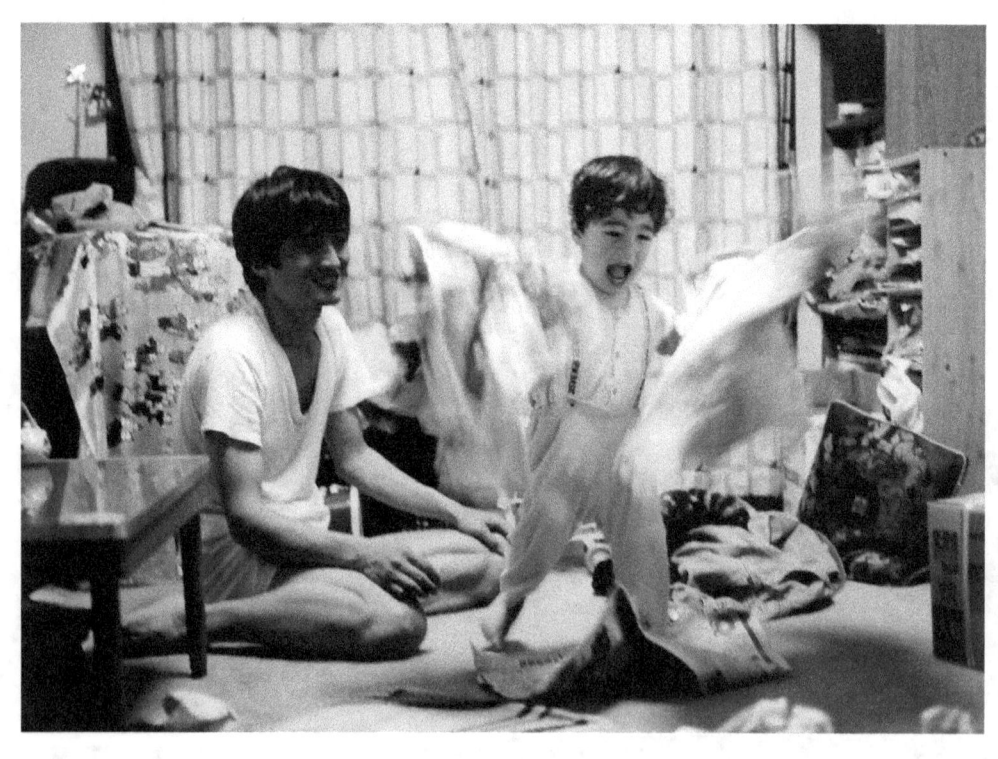

When It's All Too Much.

My Daddy says
There are so many
Sad and awful things
Happening in the world.
Wars and terrorists;
Earthquakes and floods.
Acid rain and the ozone hole.
Betrayal and hatred.
Politicians boldly telling lies,
The divide between rich and poor becoming greater.
Parents killing children,
Children stabbing children.
Newspapers are full of miserable news.

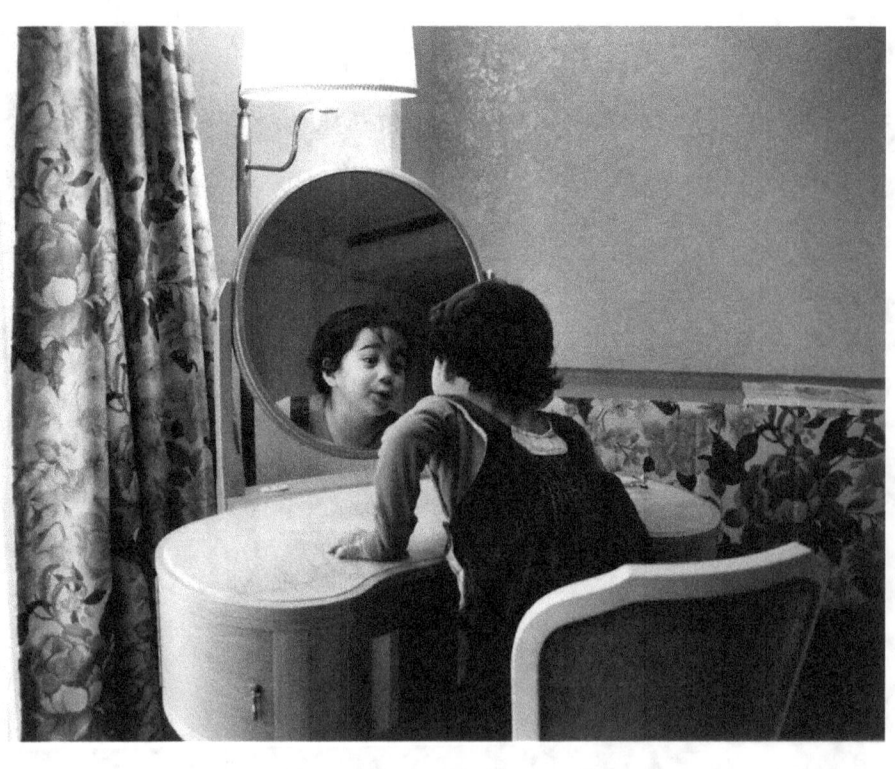

One More Me

I'm minding my own business and he suddenly appears.
What is he? Who is he?
The more I wonder the more my spine tingles.
He has huge eyes.
Maybe because his eyes
Suddenly met mine
And he was surprised.
He stares at me with pupils dilated,
Not blinking.
Even now
It seems as if he will
Swallow me with his eyes.
I'm not sure I like this anymore.

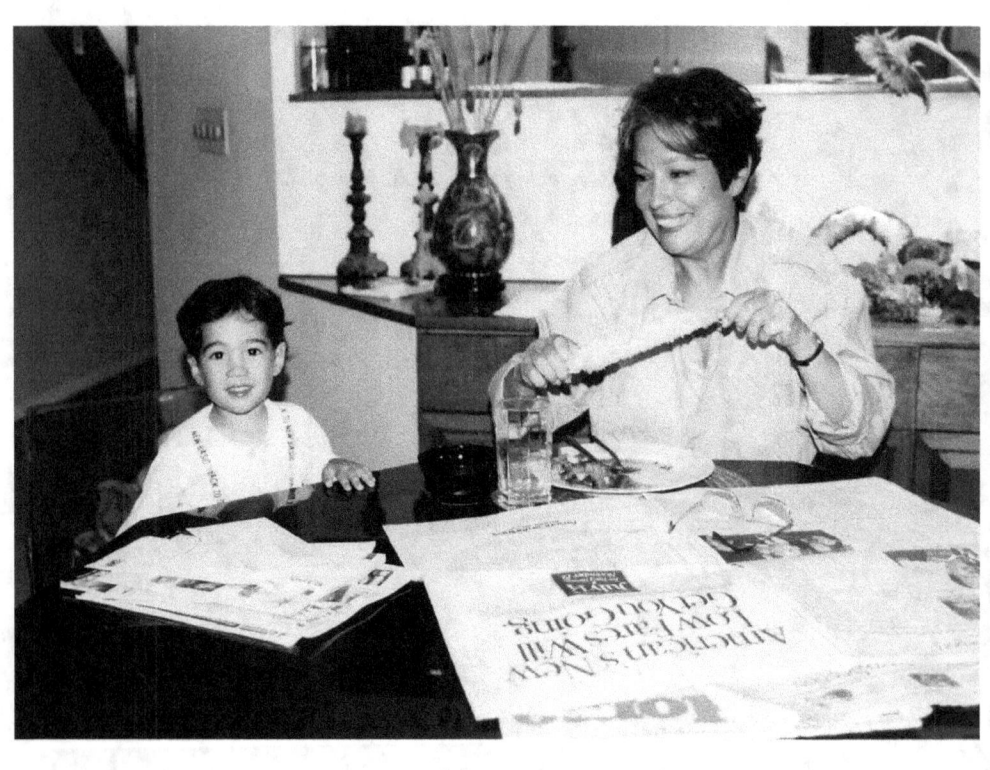

A Child's Perspective

I call my Mommy's mother
Grandma.
She's really nice but
she wears a bit too much make-up.
You should always remember.
A child's opinion
Always cuts
Deeper than
A grown-up's.
But don't misunderstand.
I love Grandma.

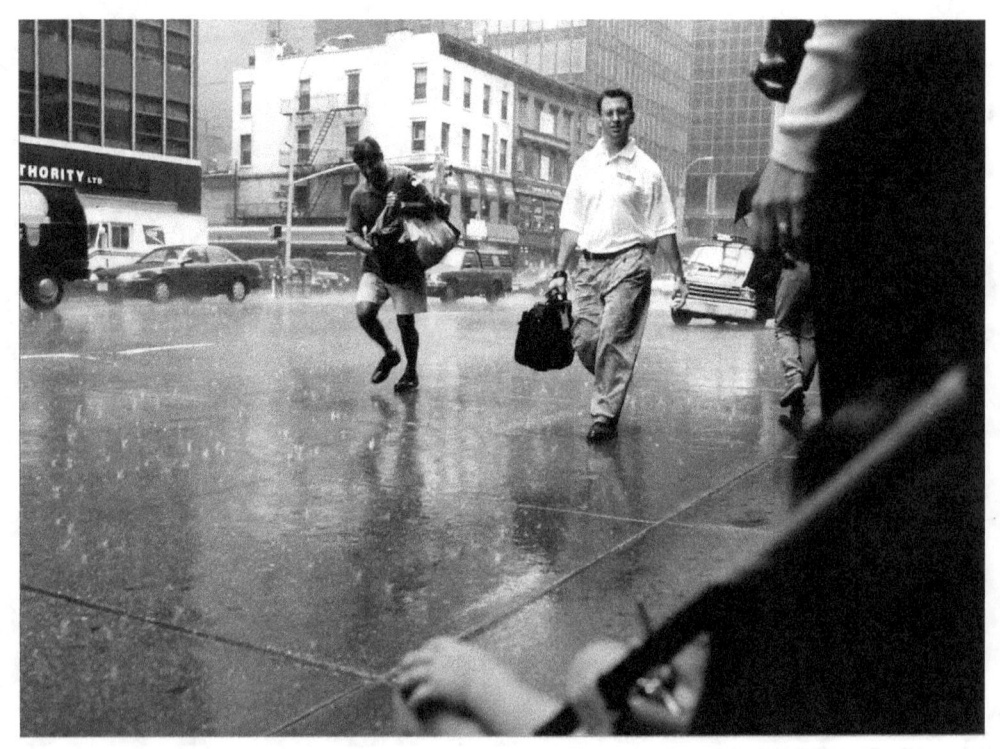

Summer Rain

The sky suddenly darkens
And raindrops the size of marbles
Come pouring down.
But you shouldn't panic.
If you start rushing and running
The next thing you know
Your feet skip out from under you
And into the muddy stream you go.
Things like that happen suddenly
On street corners in Manhattan.

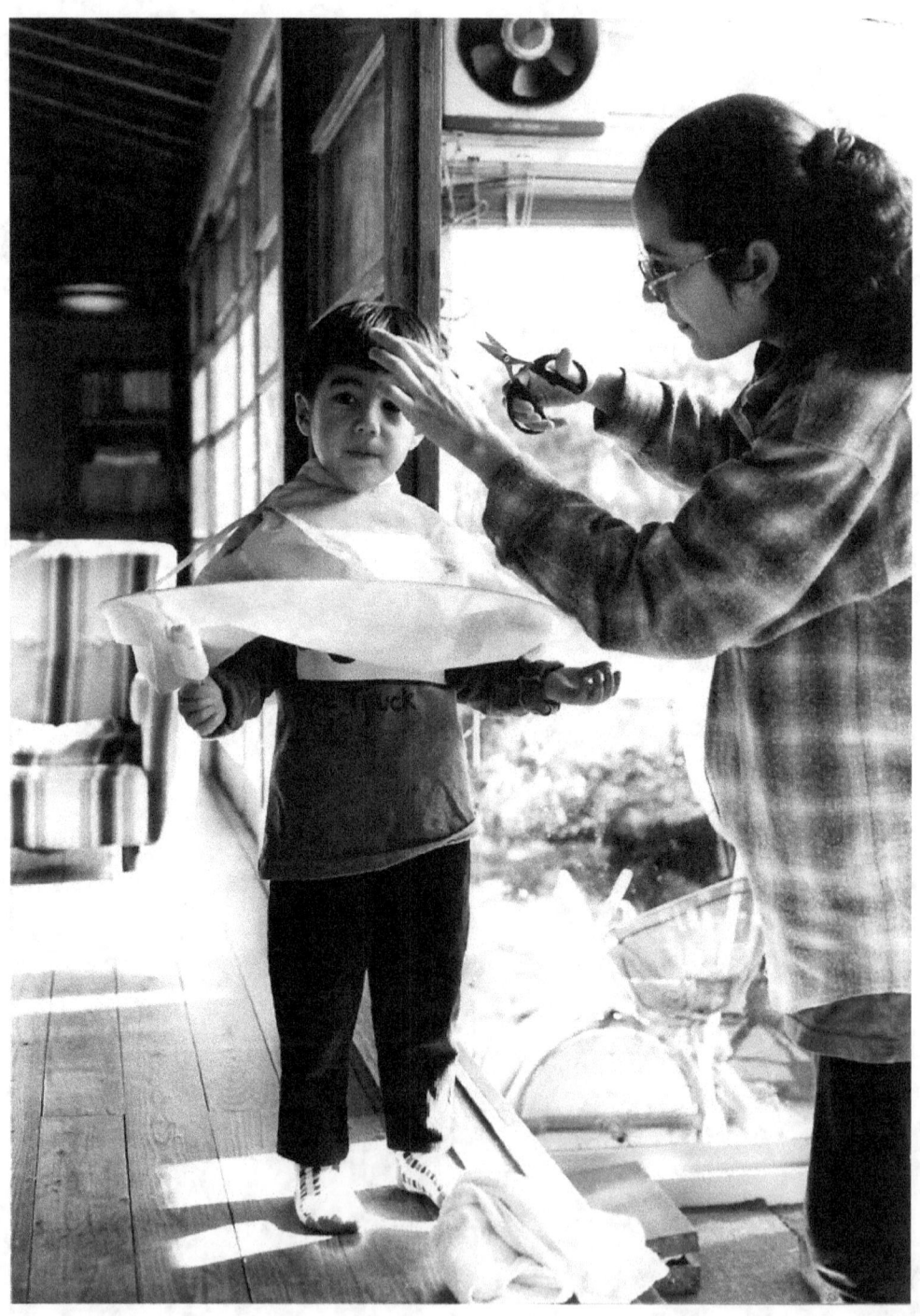

<u>Pretty neat, huh!</u>
But I guess I'm fundamentally cute, too, aren't I?

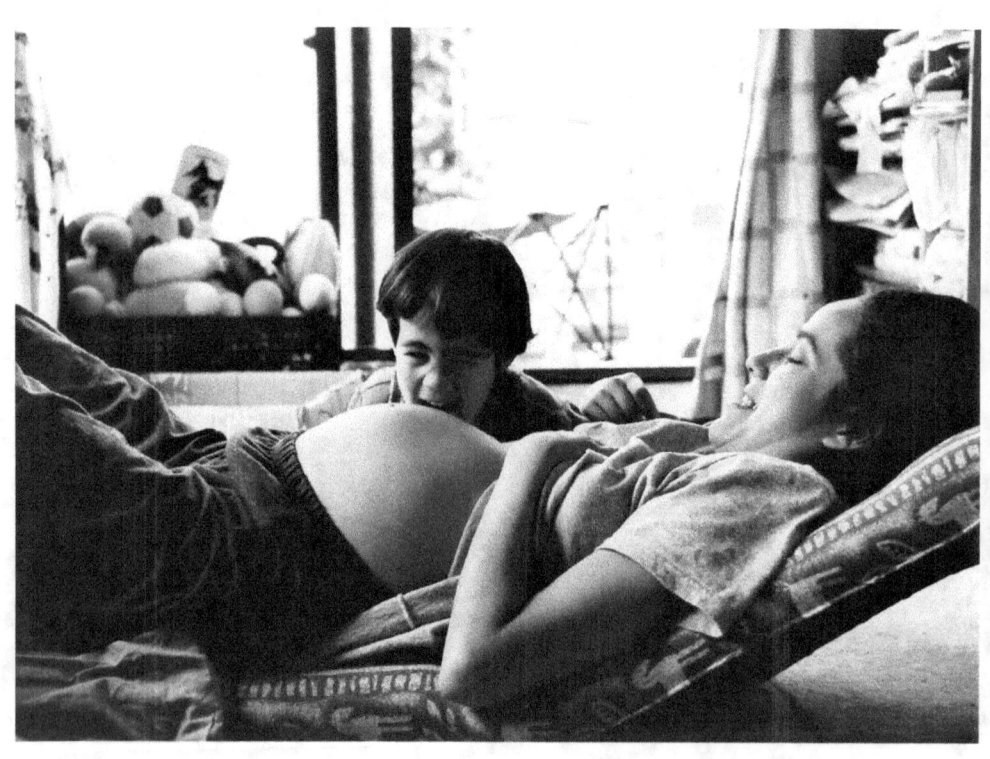

The Trap Door

Something was about to change.
I got that feeling.
But I had no idea how it was
going to affect me.
Am I expectant?
I don't know; should I be?

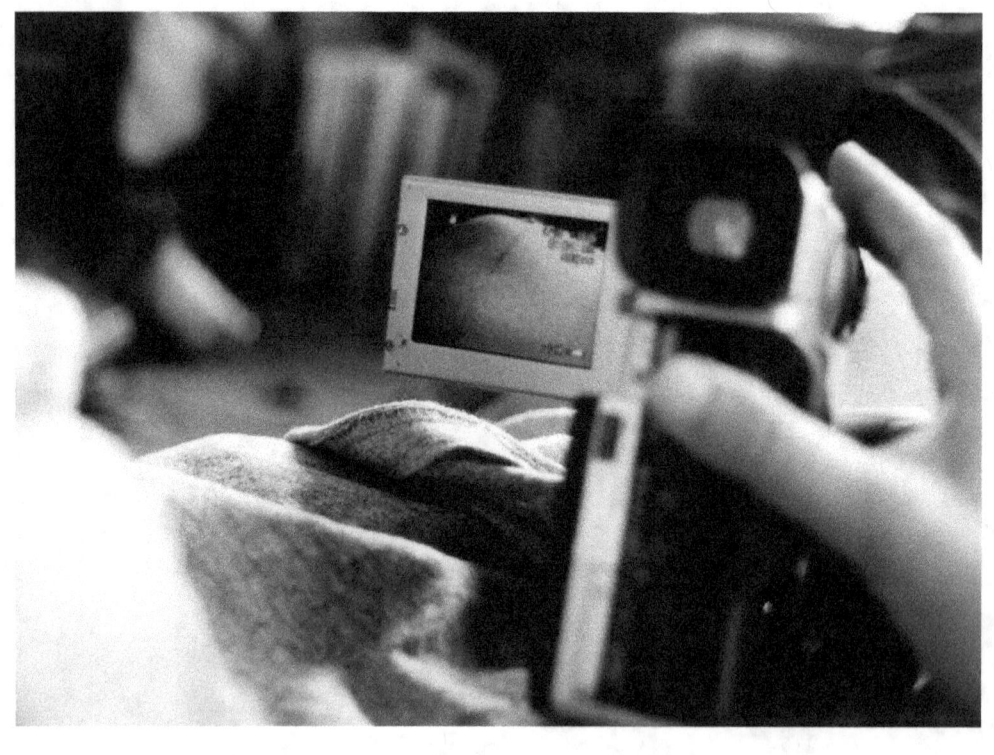

A left foot?

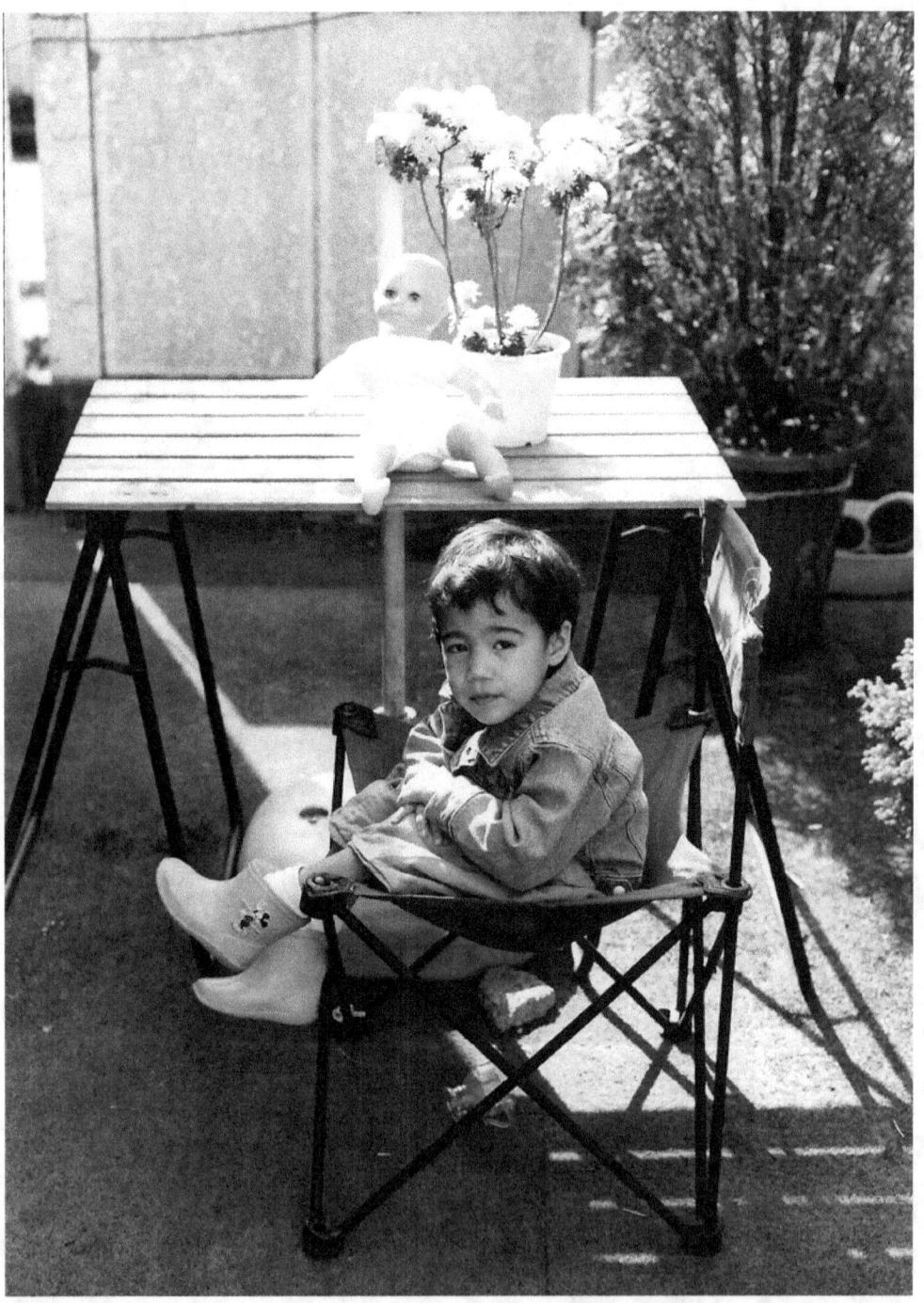

I'm Going To Be an Older Brother Soon
I don't get it.

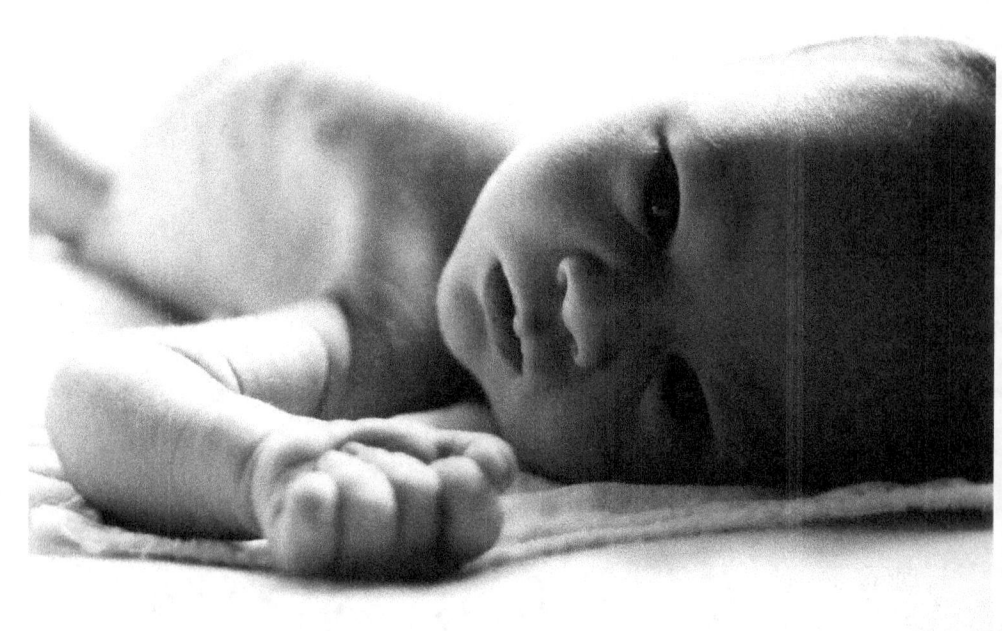

My Mommy's Daughter

My Mommy is,
Positive,
Strong willed,
Intelligent,
With a beautiful mind and body,
Cheerful,
With the emotional softness of a wooly lamb.
Maya is,
my Mommy's daughter.
Doesn't that sound good?
Wouldn't you like me to say that about you?

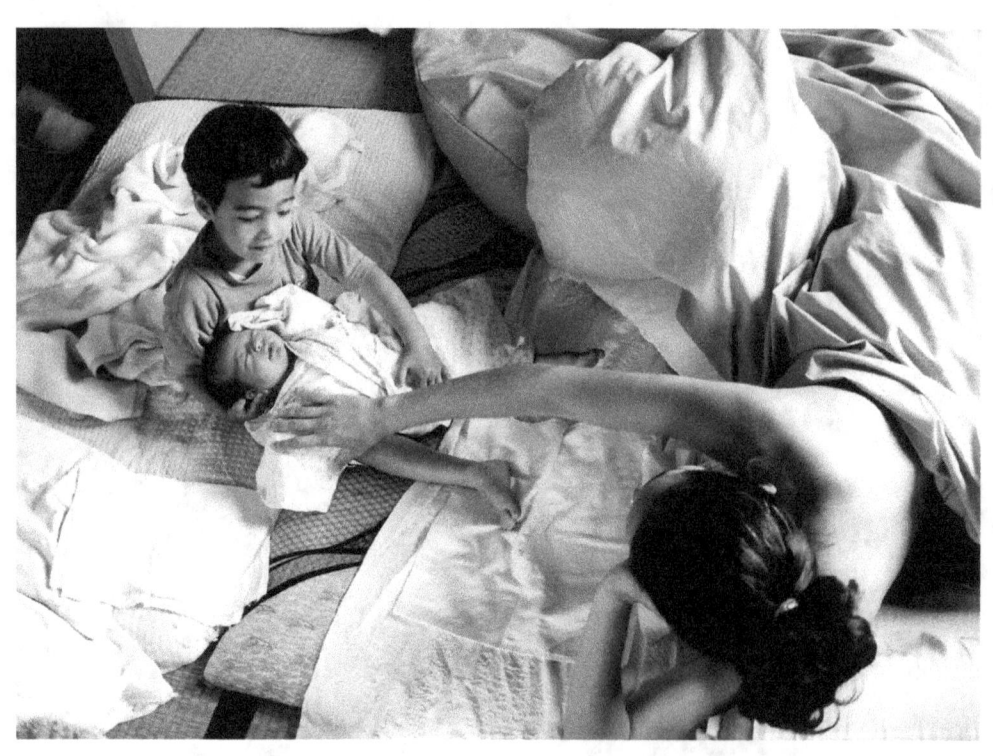

A Treasure

What is there to say?
She fascinates me.

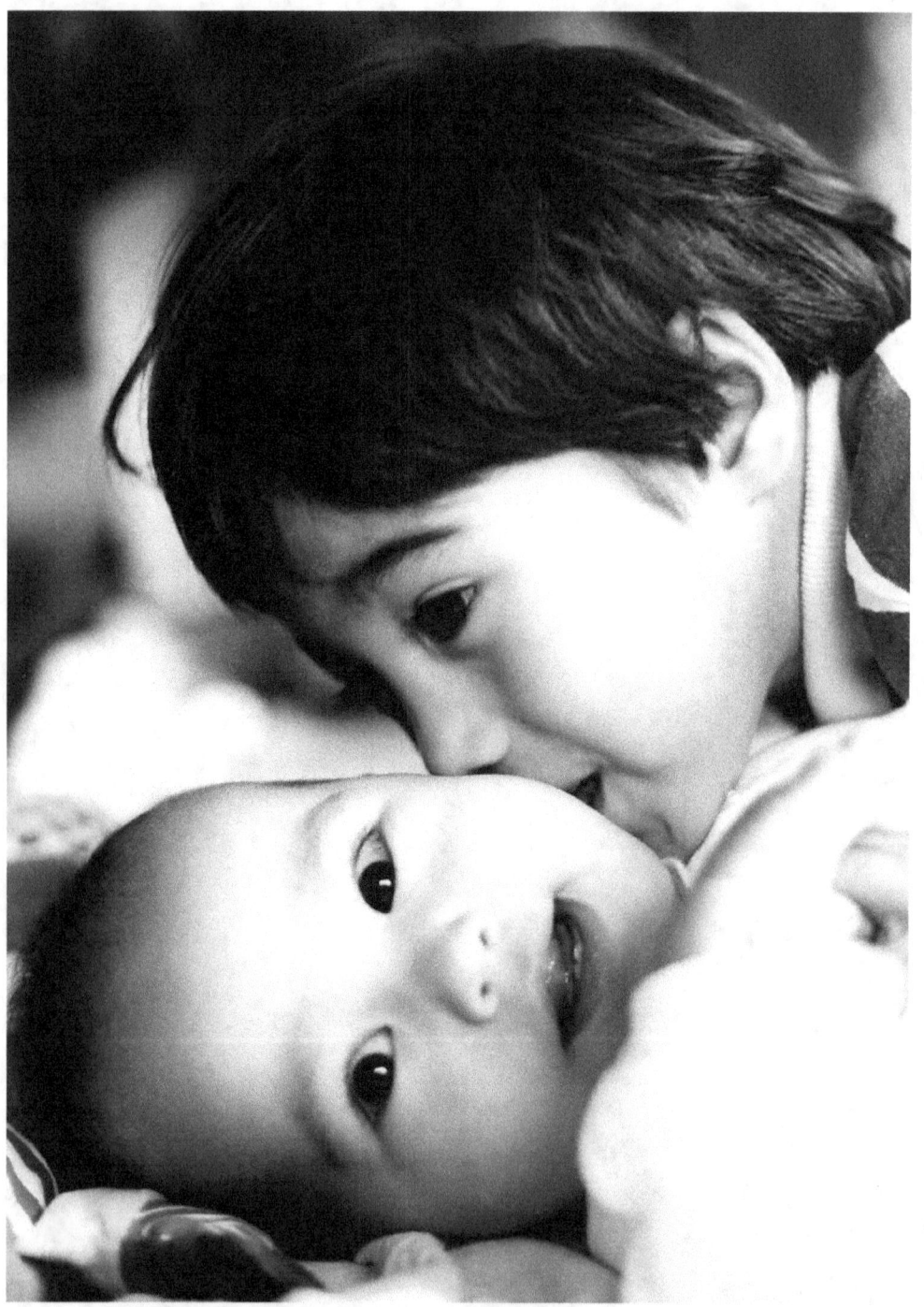

Scent
Maya smells sooooo good.

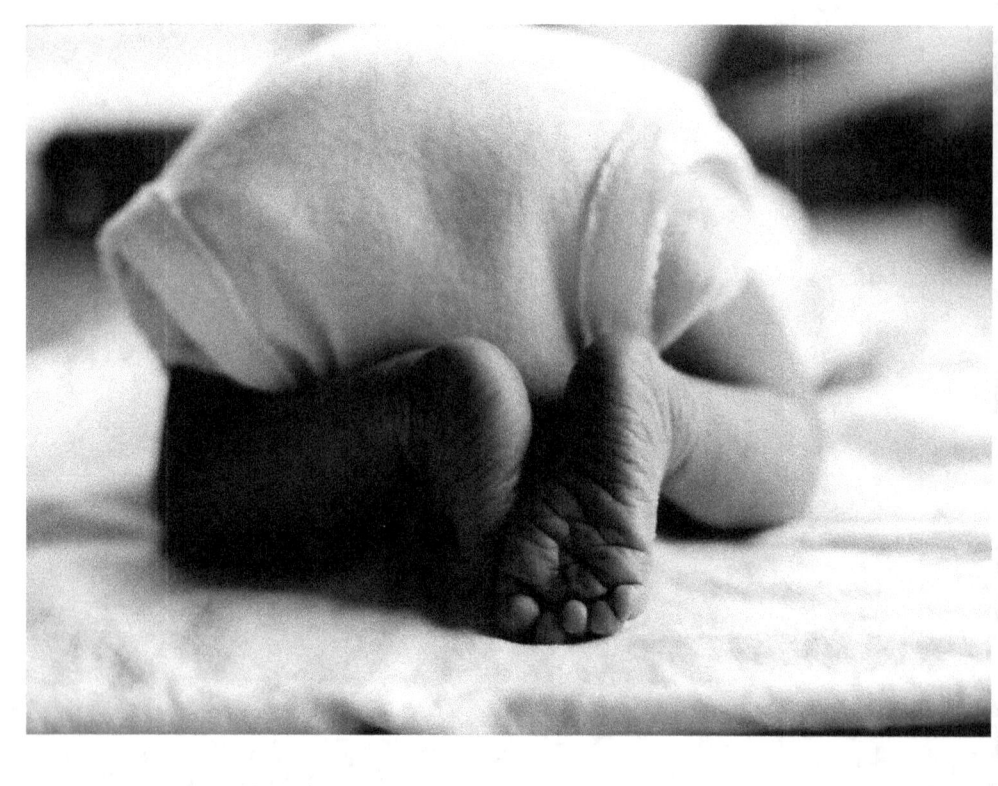

Softness
Don't you just want to touch it?

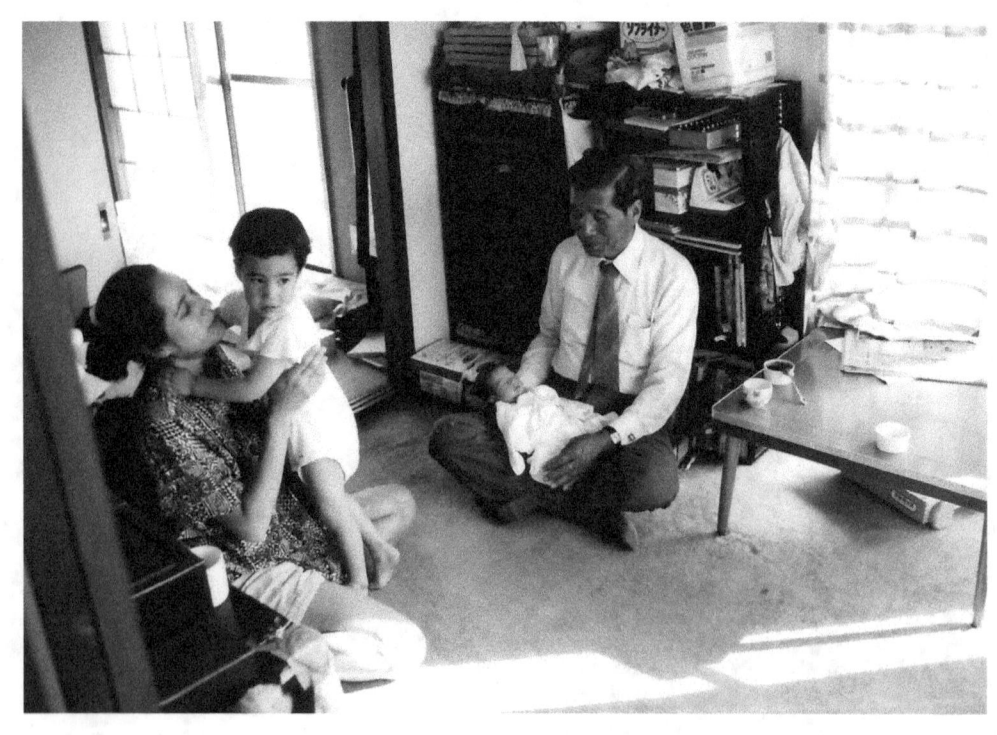

Sei-chan

Yes, I call him Sei-chan.

Daddy's father.

And why not? Mommy and Daddy have always called him that.

It's fine, don't you think?

His face is a bit dark, his voice loud.

Once in a while, he's a bit scary.

But really, he isn't at all.

Whenever we climb Mt. Tsukuba,

he always carries me on his back to the top.

Of course Maya, too!

Ah yes, because by that time,

I, the older brother, was walking.

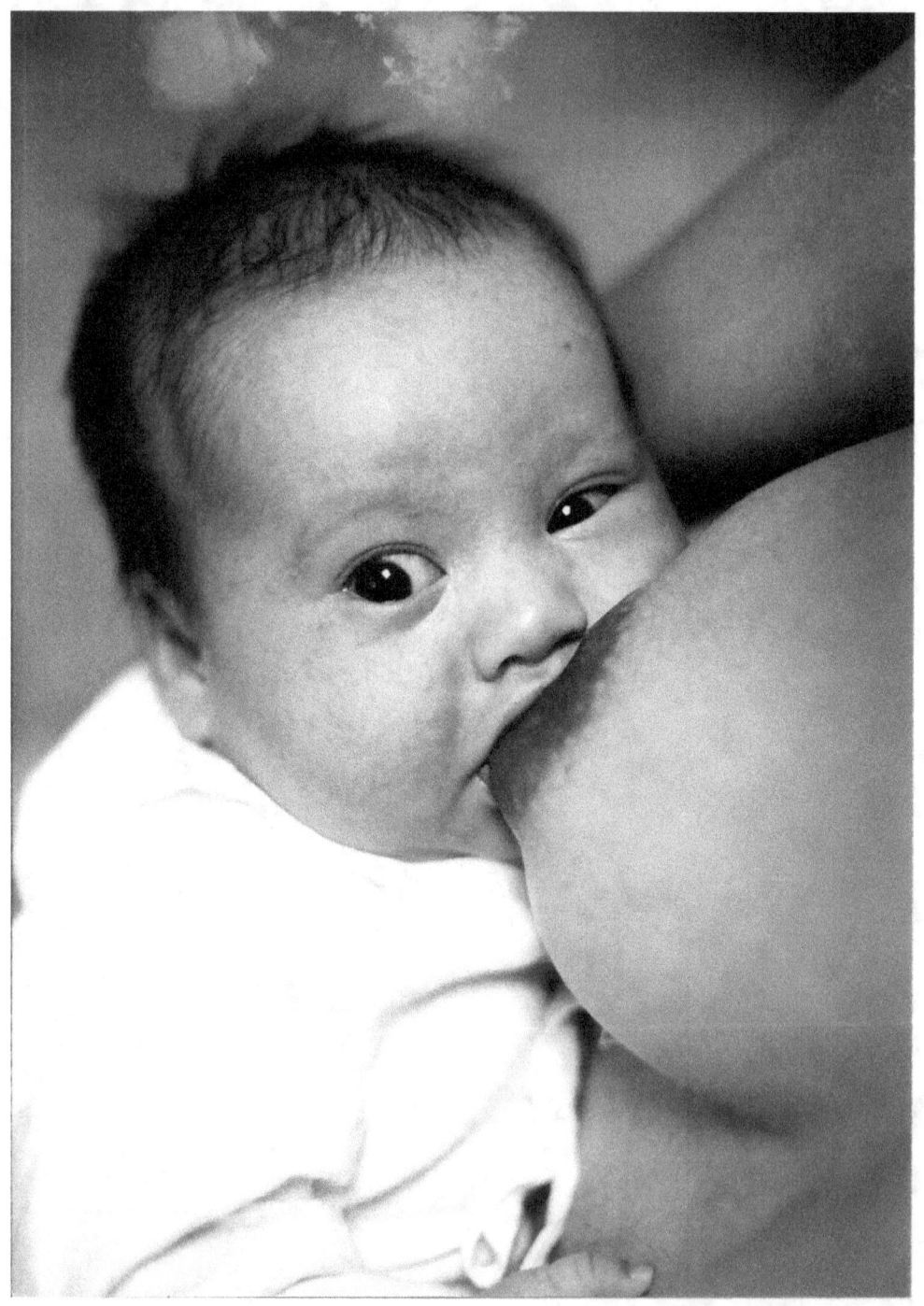

Dethroned
Maya! Take turns!

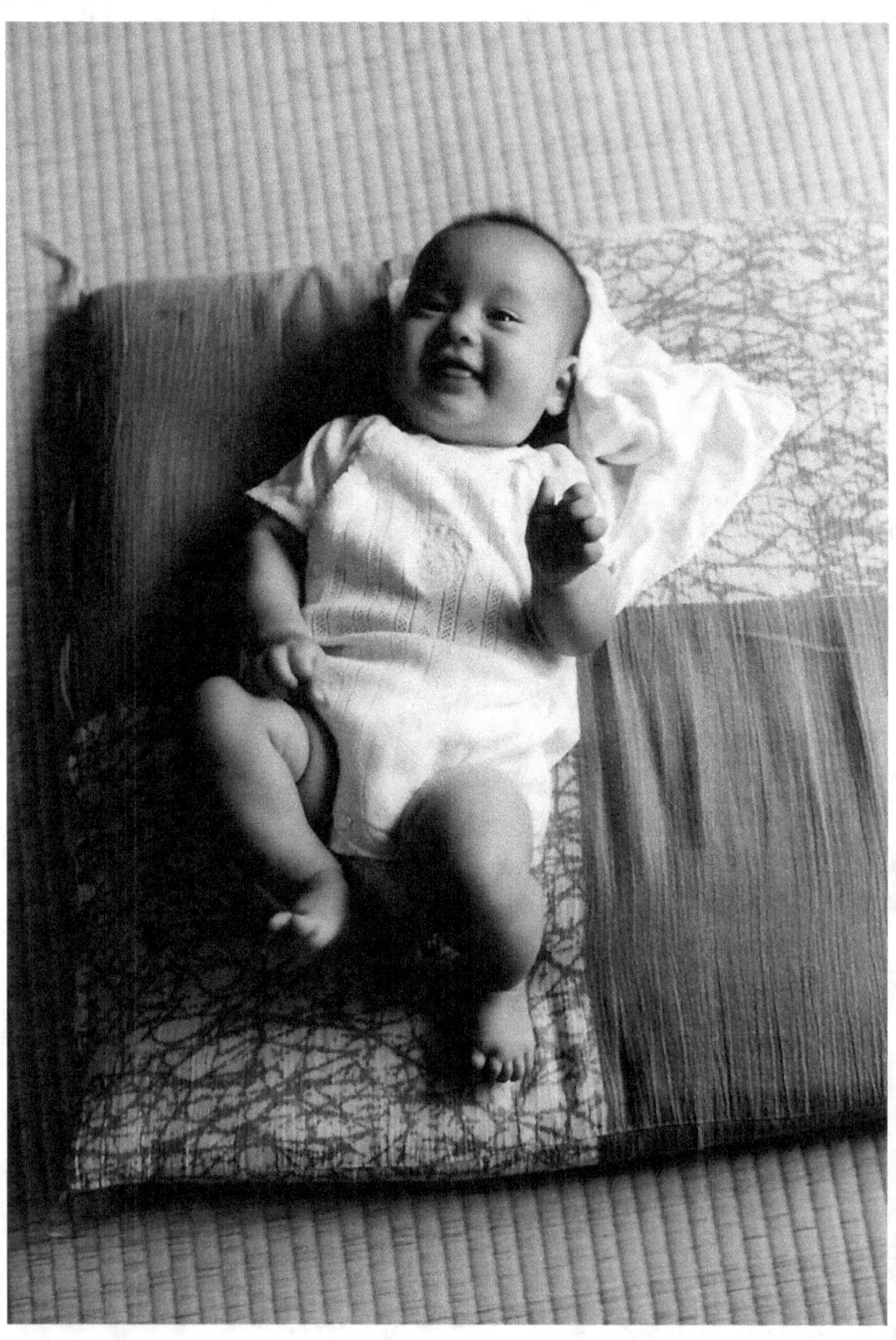

Cushions are a bit special
Cool to the touch,
They feel so cozy.

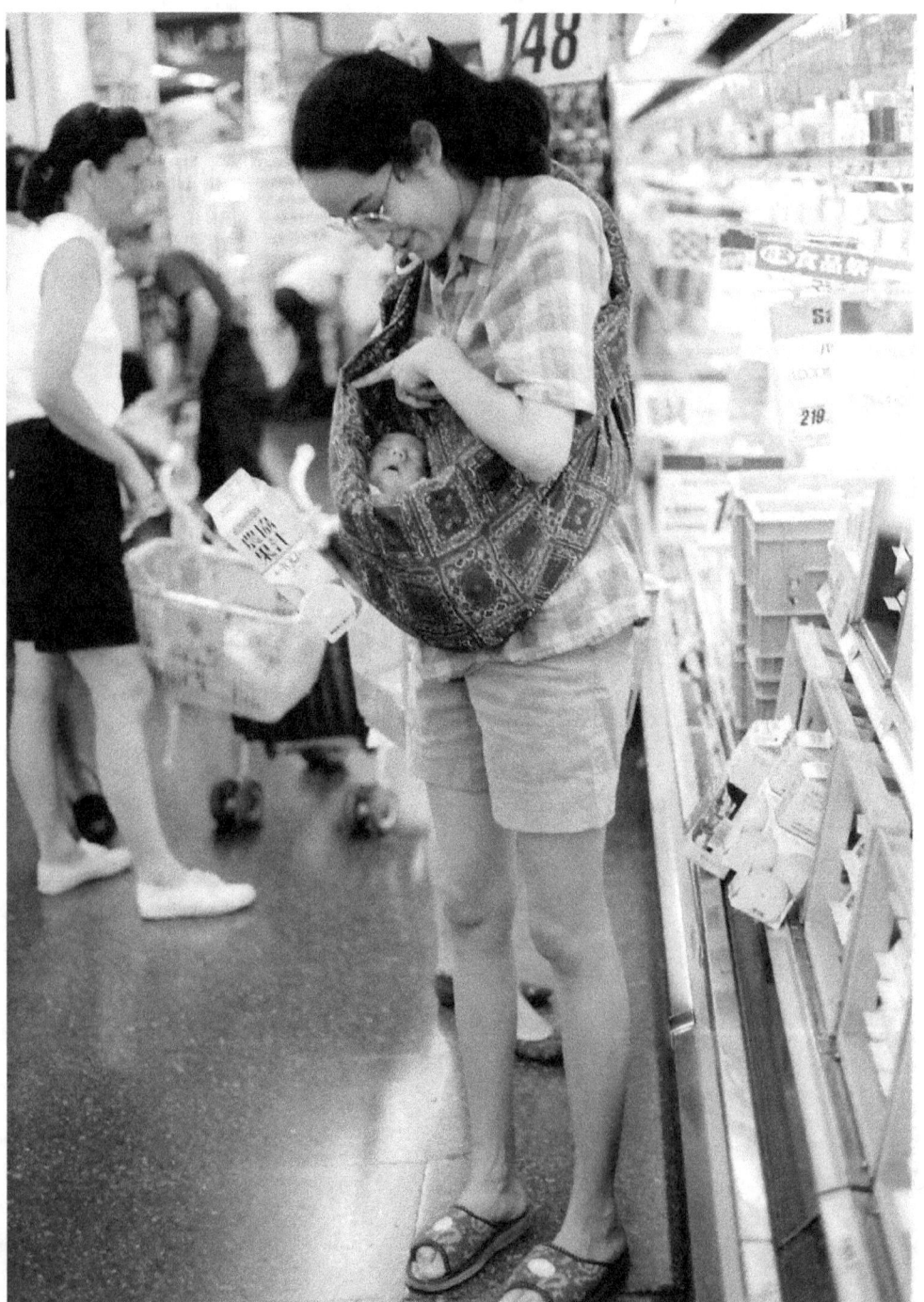

What Is Normal?

I hate the word "normal."
I always hear it
But what does it mean?
Not special…
Excuse me?!
A normal child,
a normal parent,
a normal family,
There is no such thing.
Someone who couldn't be bothered
must have thought up that word.
We should get rid of it.
Then, everyone could be real.

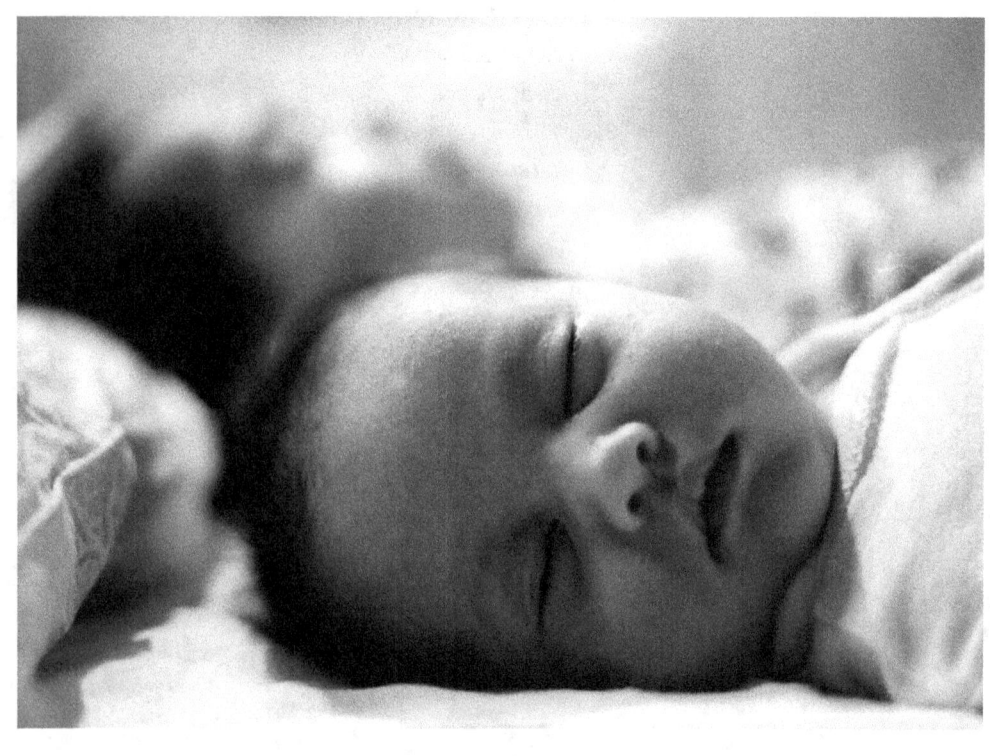

The Freedom to Dream
Now is the time
All dreams
Can come true.

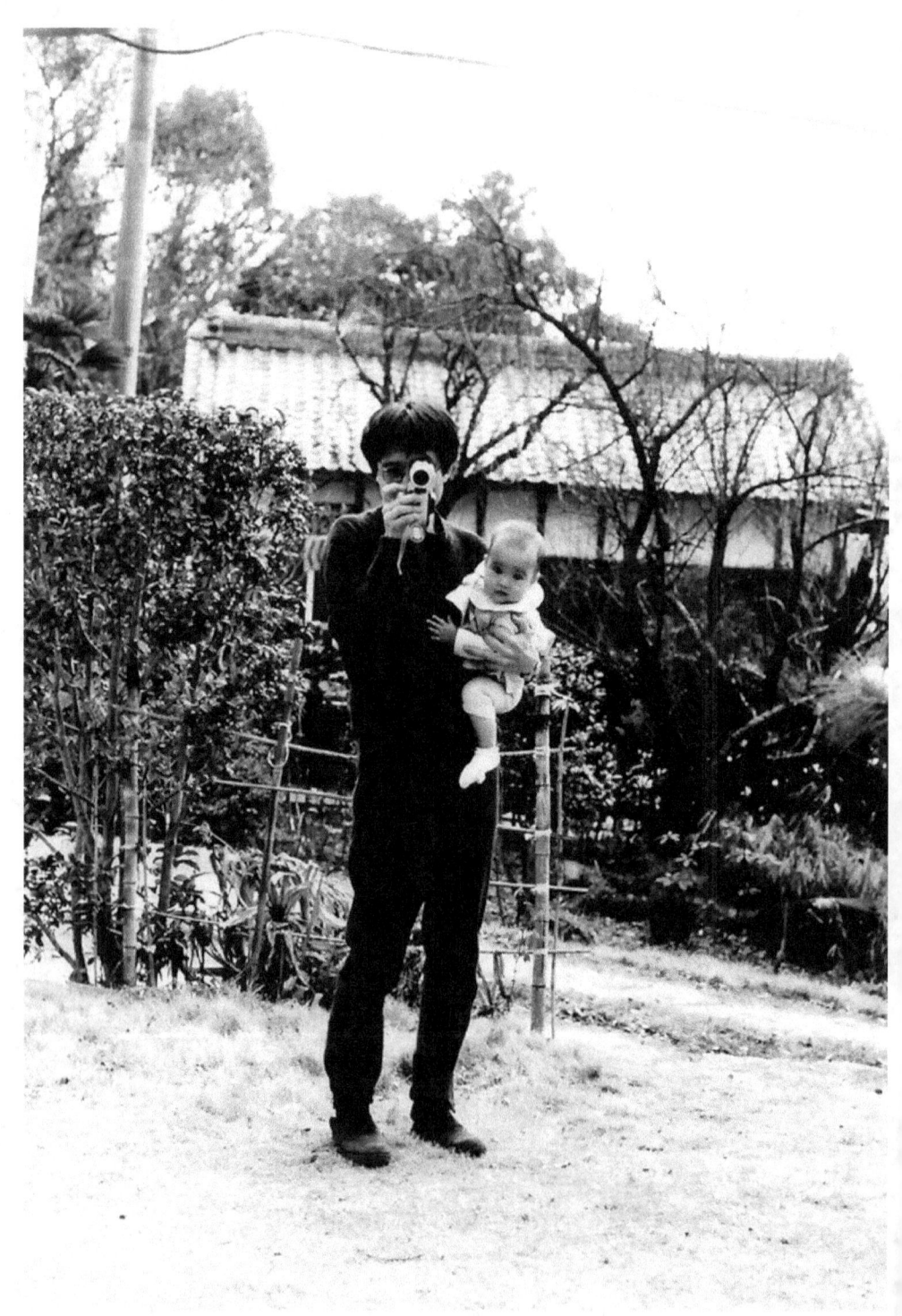

<u>Huggy Baby?</u>

Maya is like a little huggy baby doll.
See! She's stuck to Daddy again.

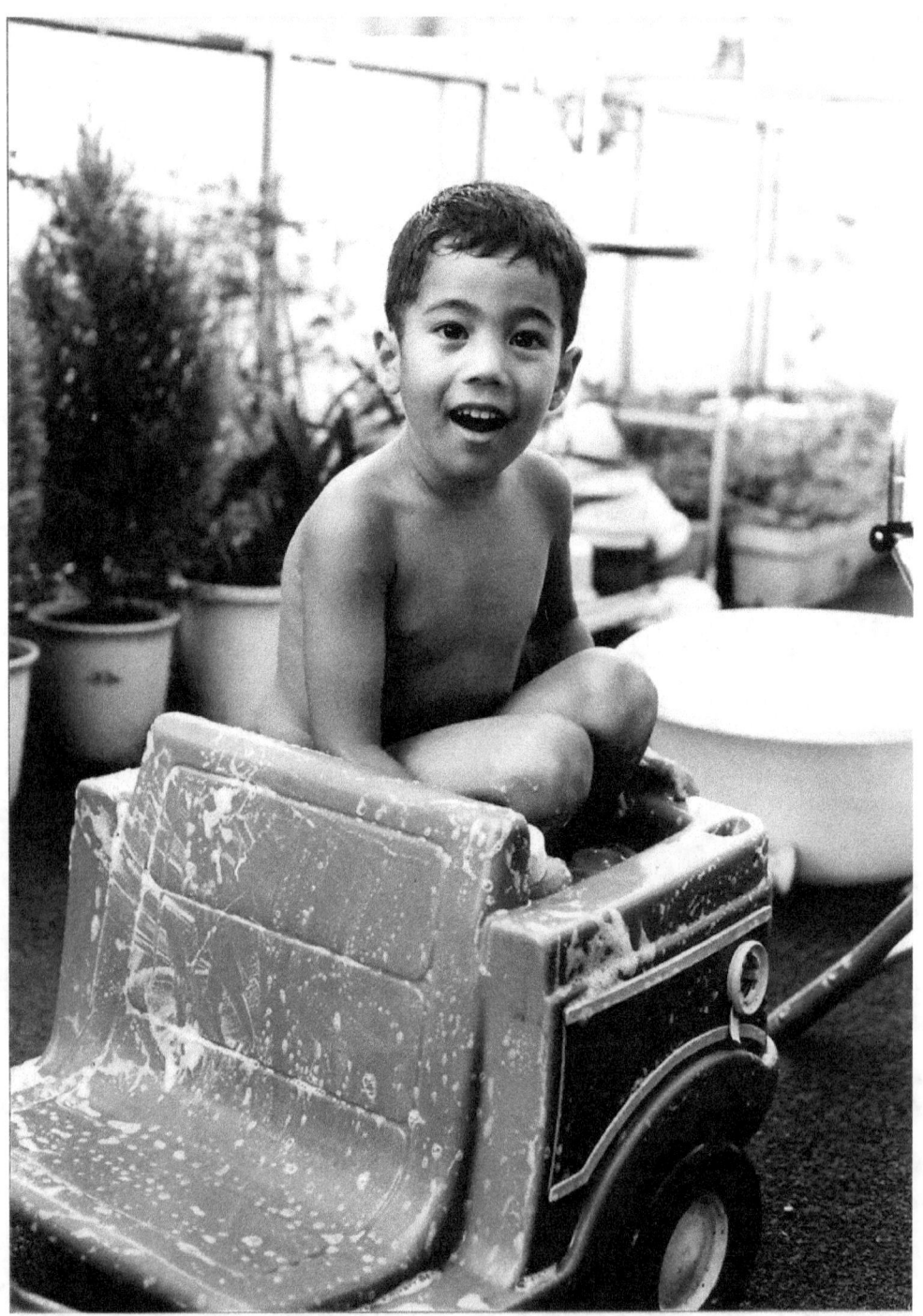

Growing Up
"Hey,
I didn't cry once today…"
As soon as I realized that
Sadness overcame me.

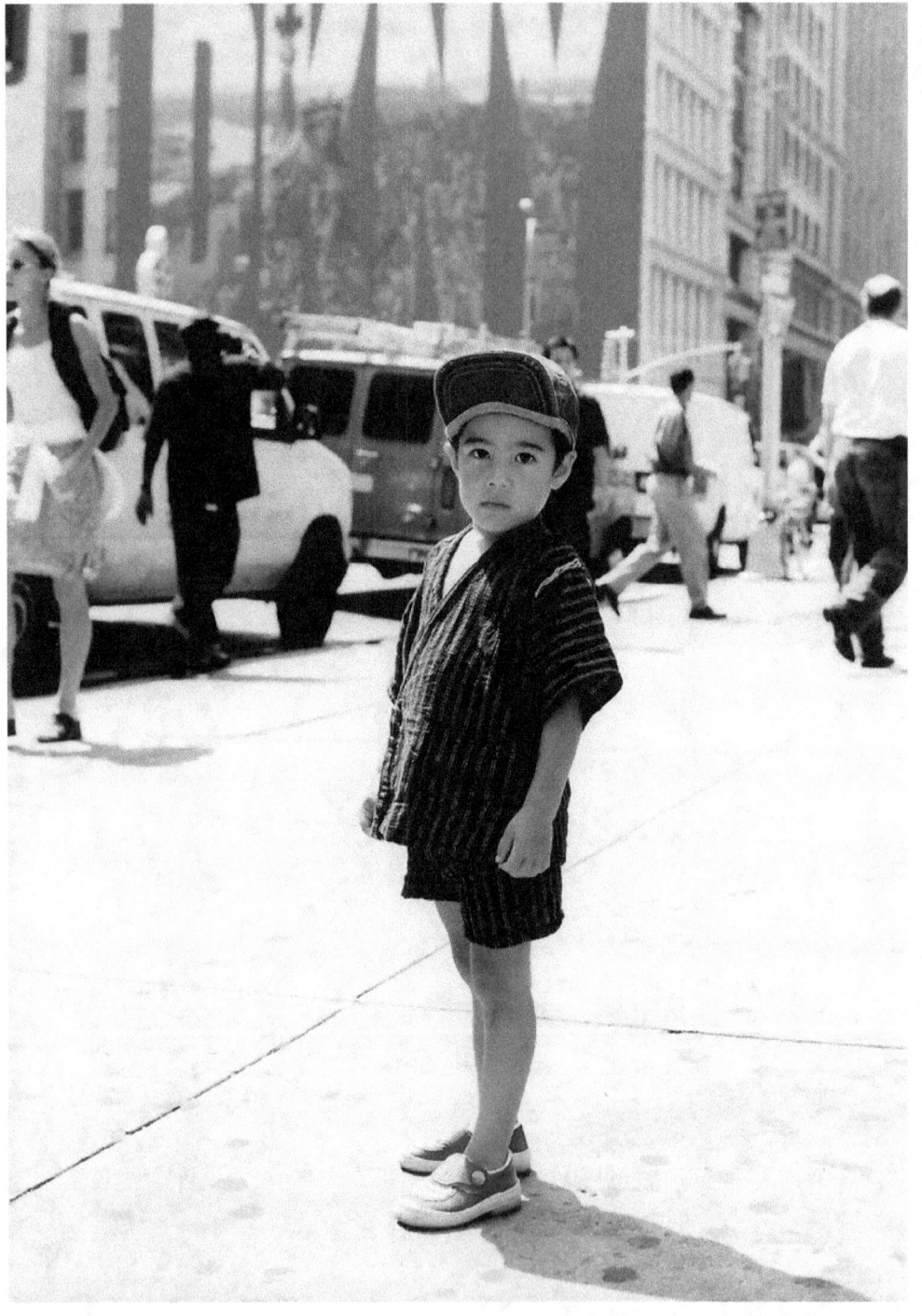

Japanese Style in NY

This outfit is called a jinbei.

It's nice, isn't it?

Kind of cool.

A bit rascally.

Awesome!

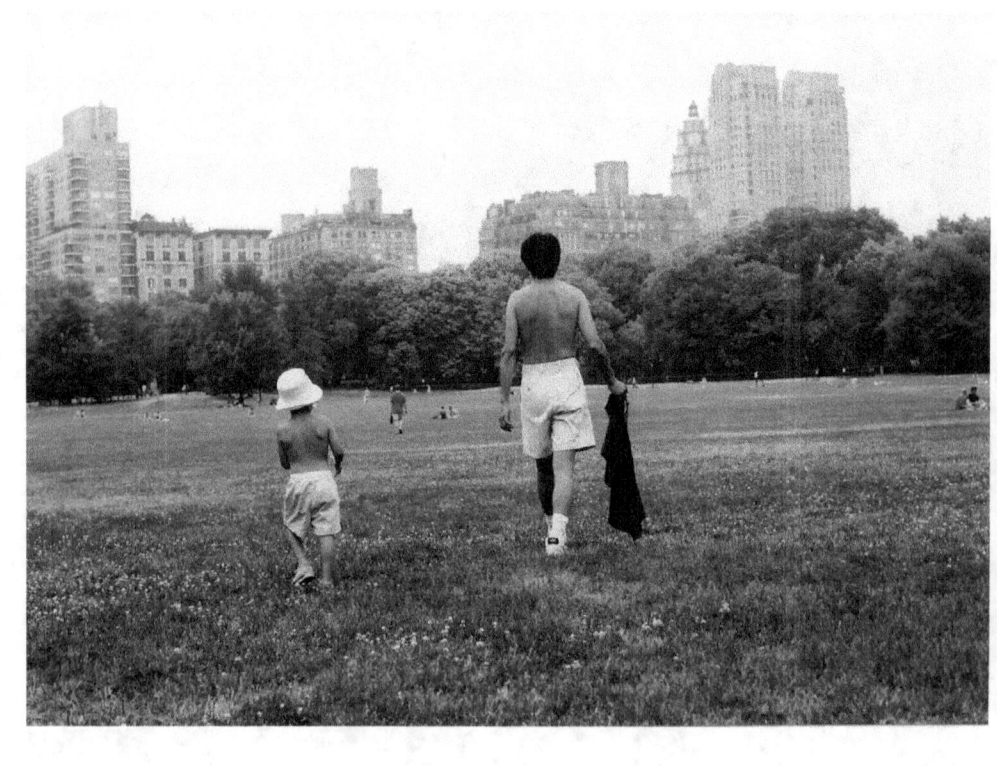

<u>Dear Statue of Liberty</u>

I have a question.
What will become of me?
When I become like my Daddy,
What will my Daddy become?
What about Mommy?
And Maya?

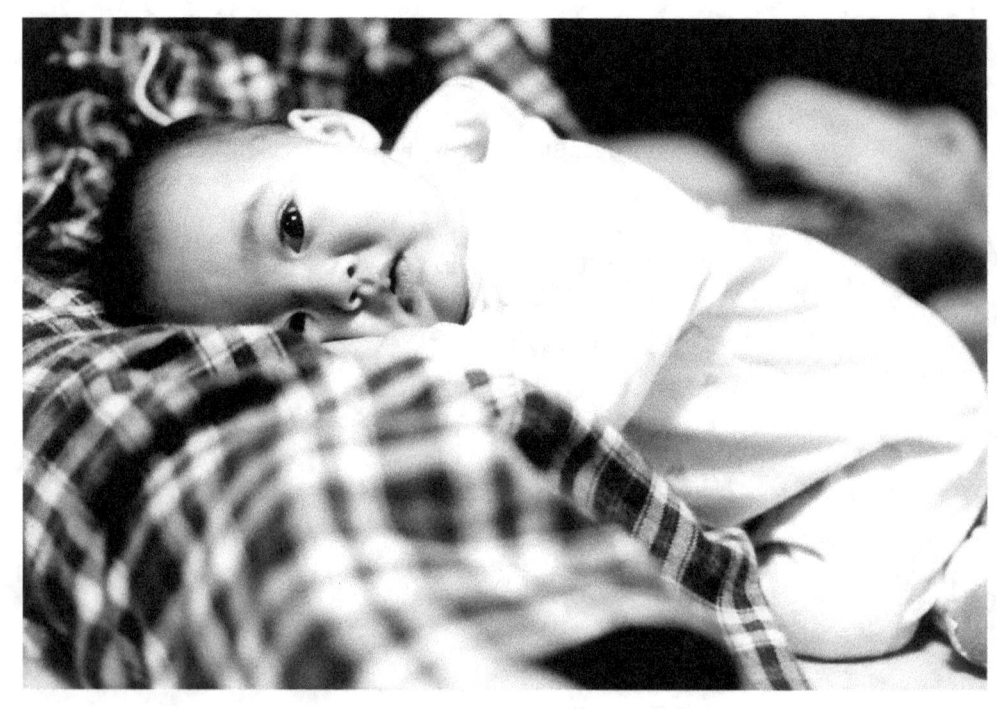

As Is

Freedom is the cornerstone of the future.
What are you looking at?
The future?

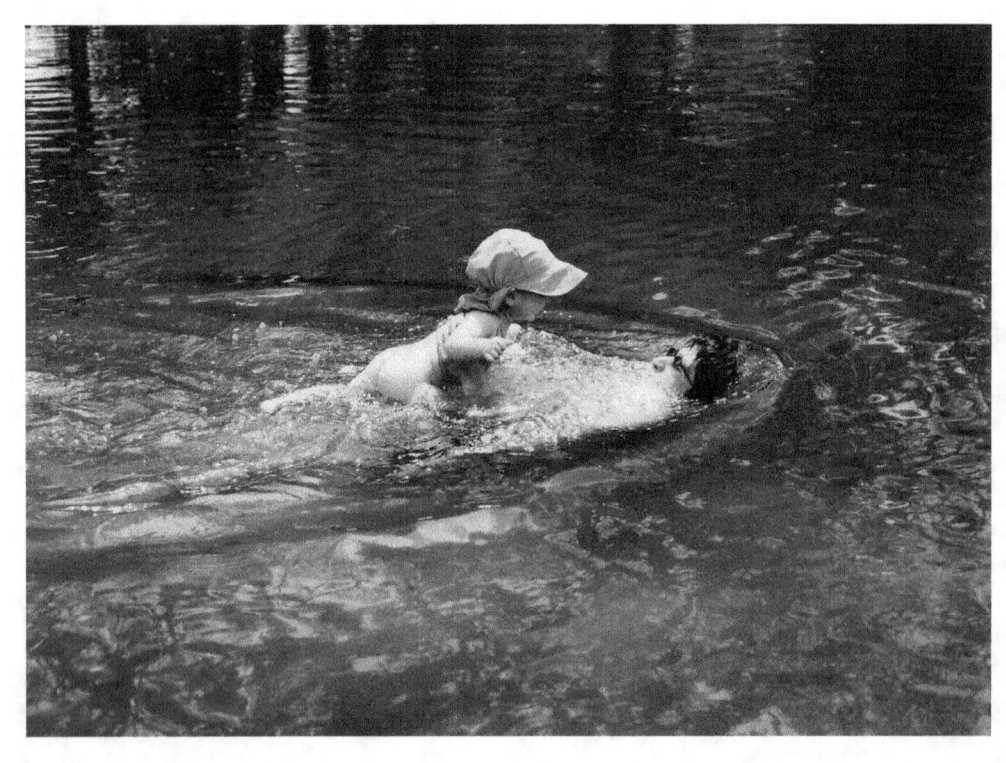

From Experience
I know
What happens next.
You go under water.
Oh my God!

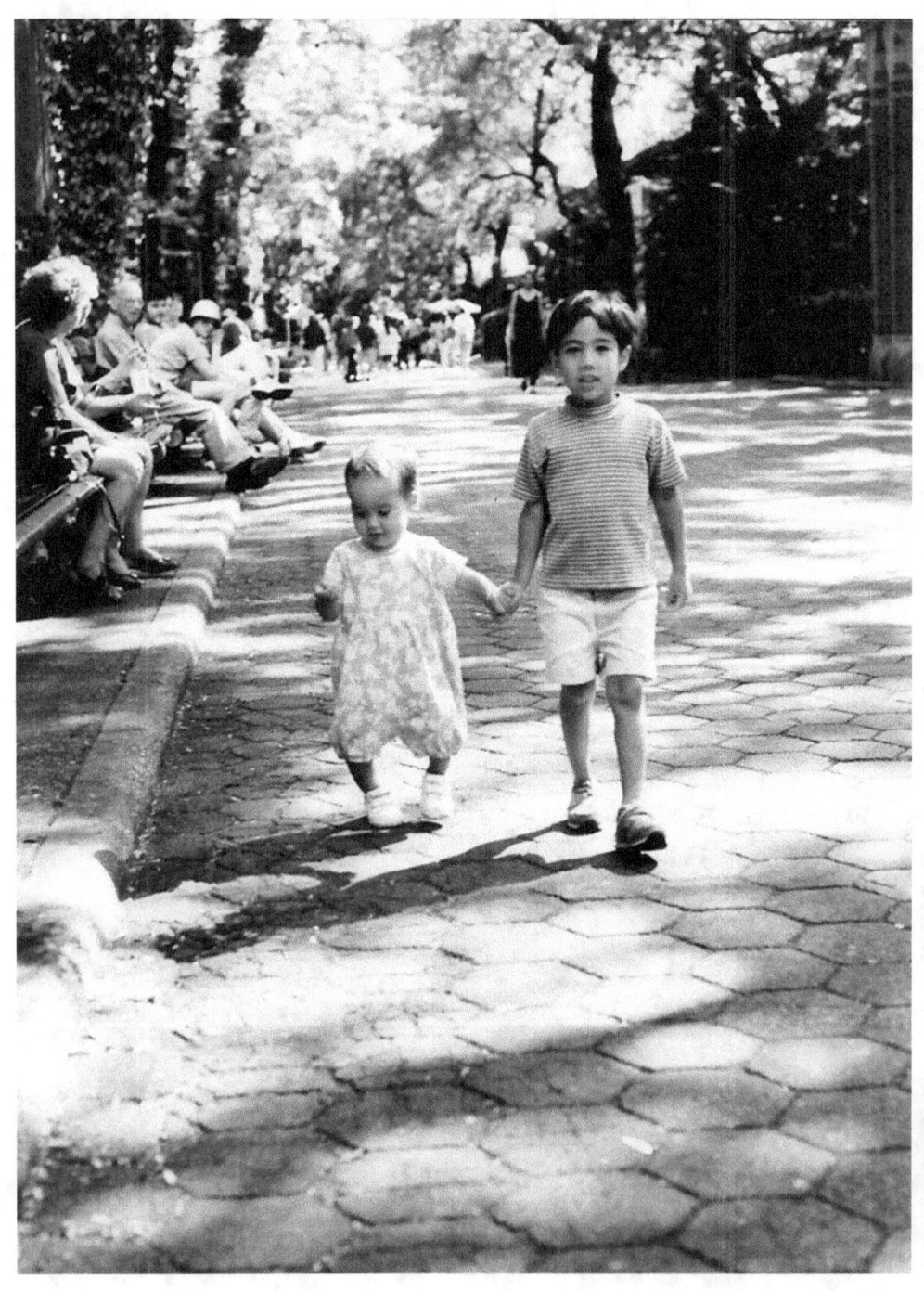

Our Street

Holding hands.
Why?
So Maya doesn't fall?
Maybe.
So that I don't fall?
Nope.
I realized,
We were simply holding hands.
Our street.
We can walk forever.
Holding hands we steadily walk apace.
Hey Maya, are you listening?

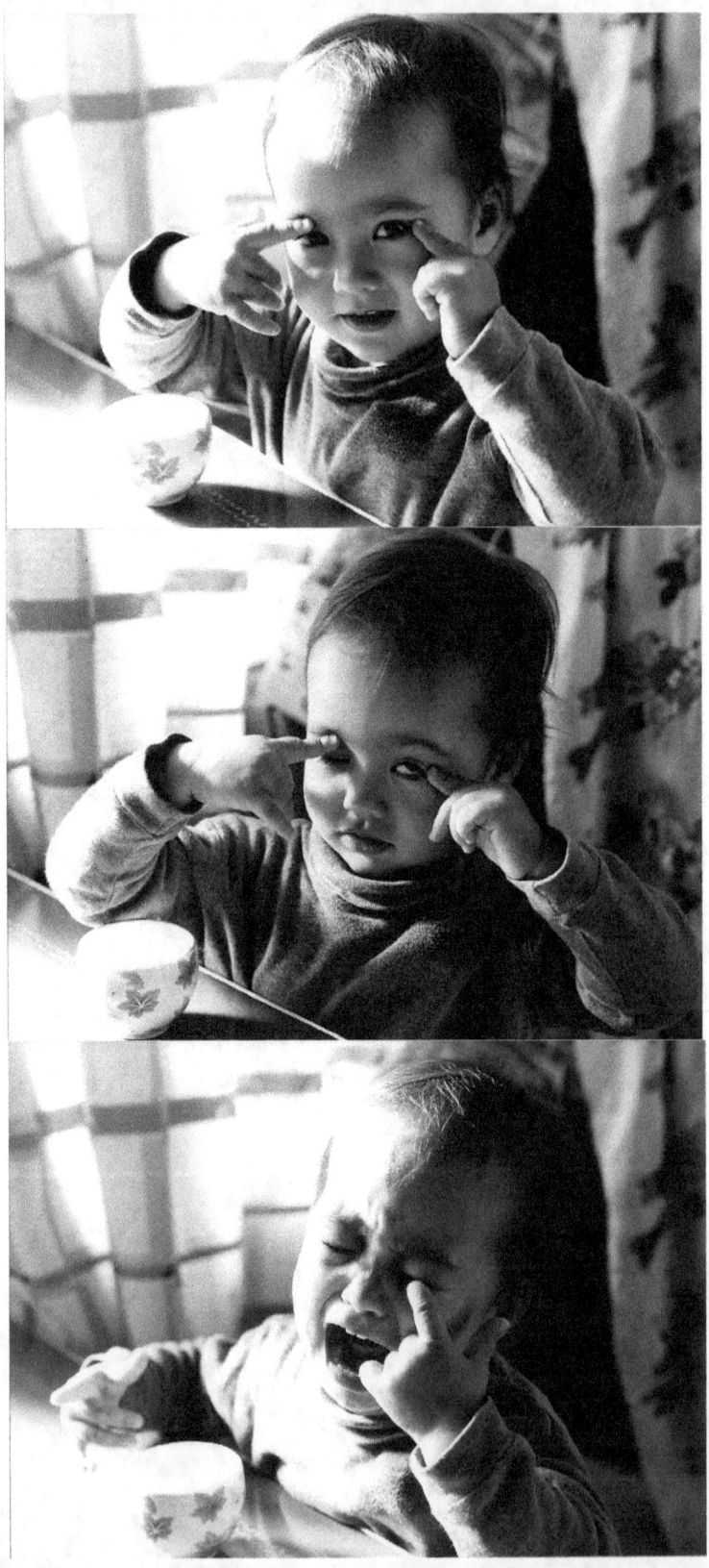

A Reason For Crying

You don't know, do you?
One minute for Mommy and Daddy
Is like 2 or 3 hours for us.
That's why we cry
If we are left alone.

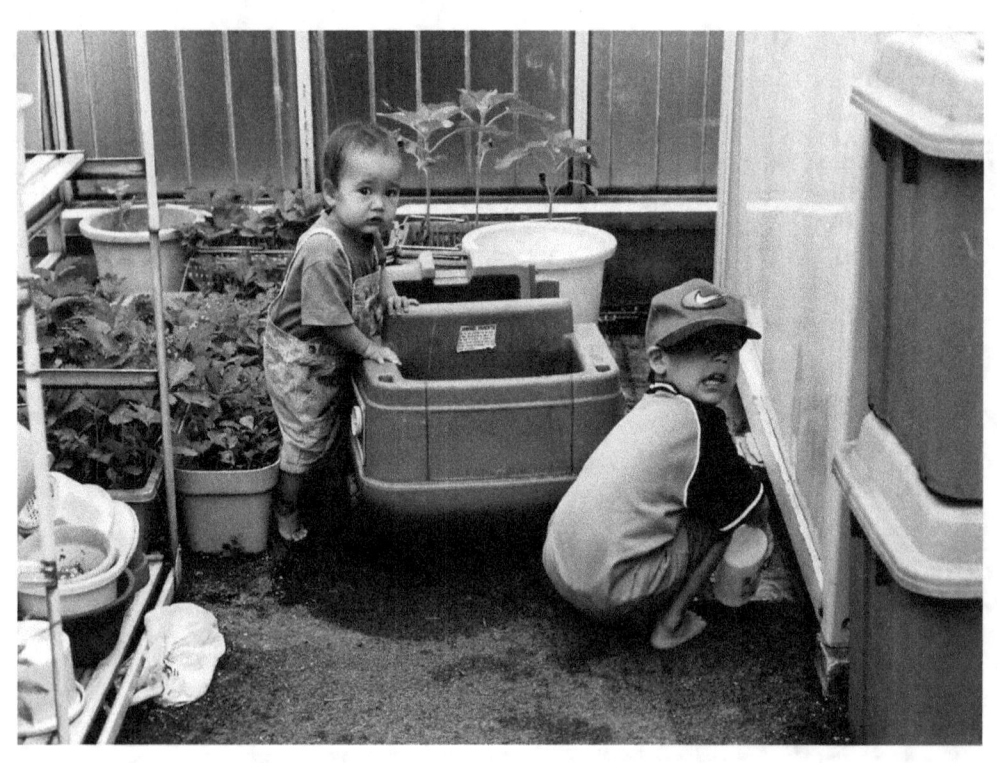

What?
"Can you tell us
what Maya just said?"
Mommy and Daddy
Always ask me that.
"Waaaaa!"
That's all Maya said.

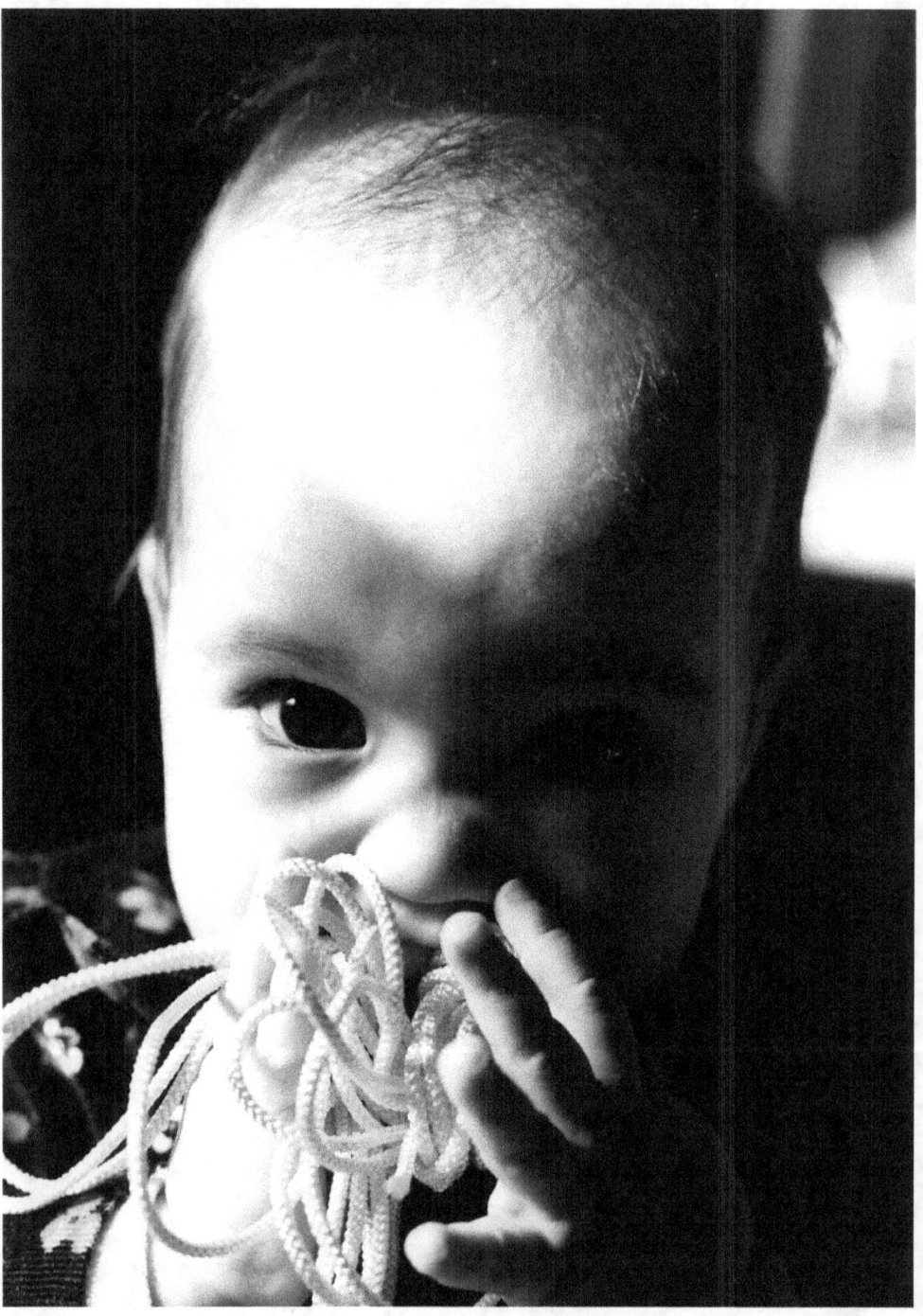

Her Pupils

Did you know
That a person's eyes
Never change?
That means that even
When Maya is a
Wrinkly old lady
Her eyes will be just
As they are now.
Do you believe that?
Well, I do.

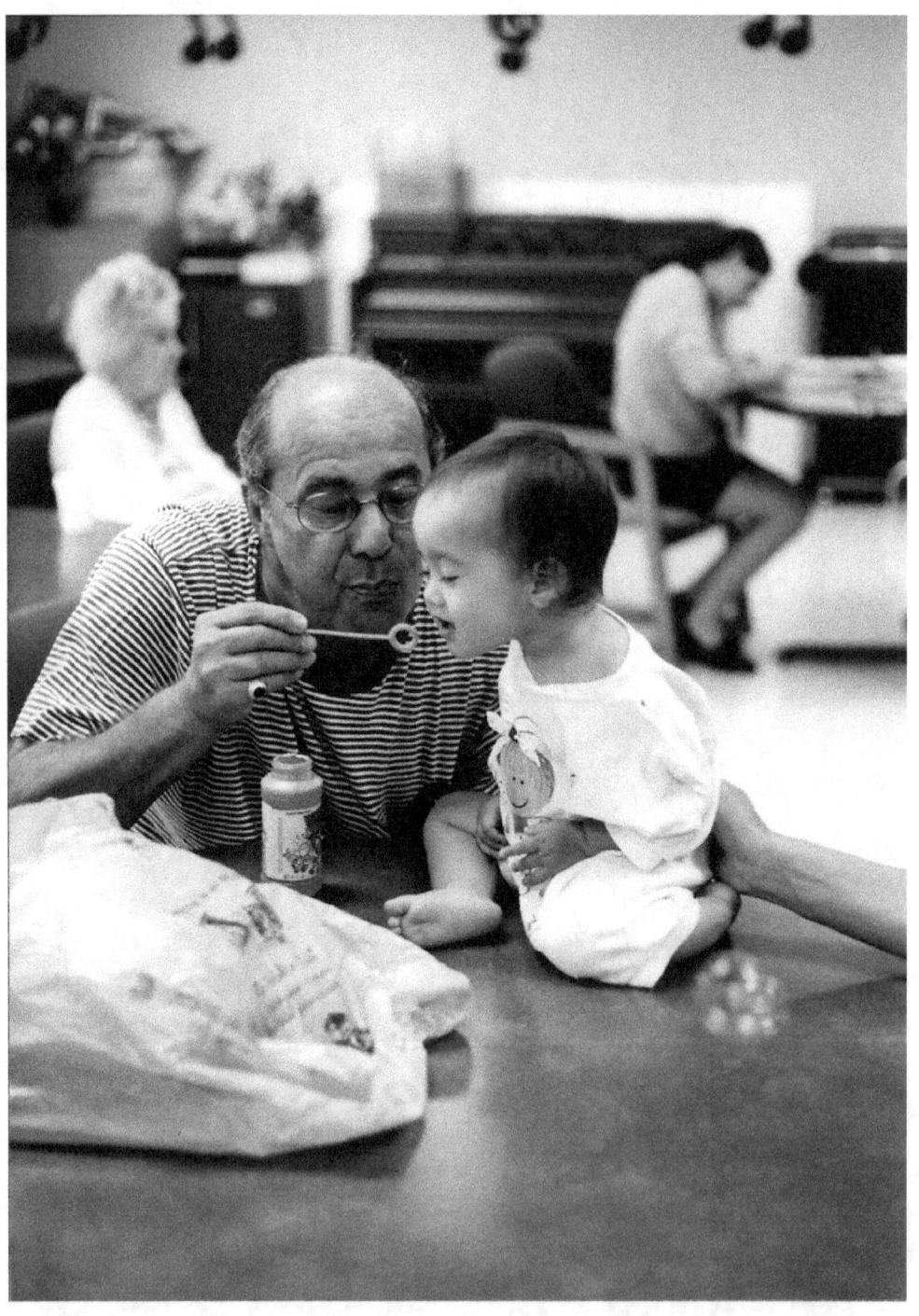

<u>Affection</u>

Maya is
Charming in that way.

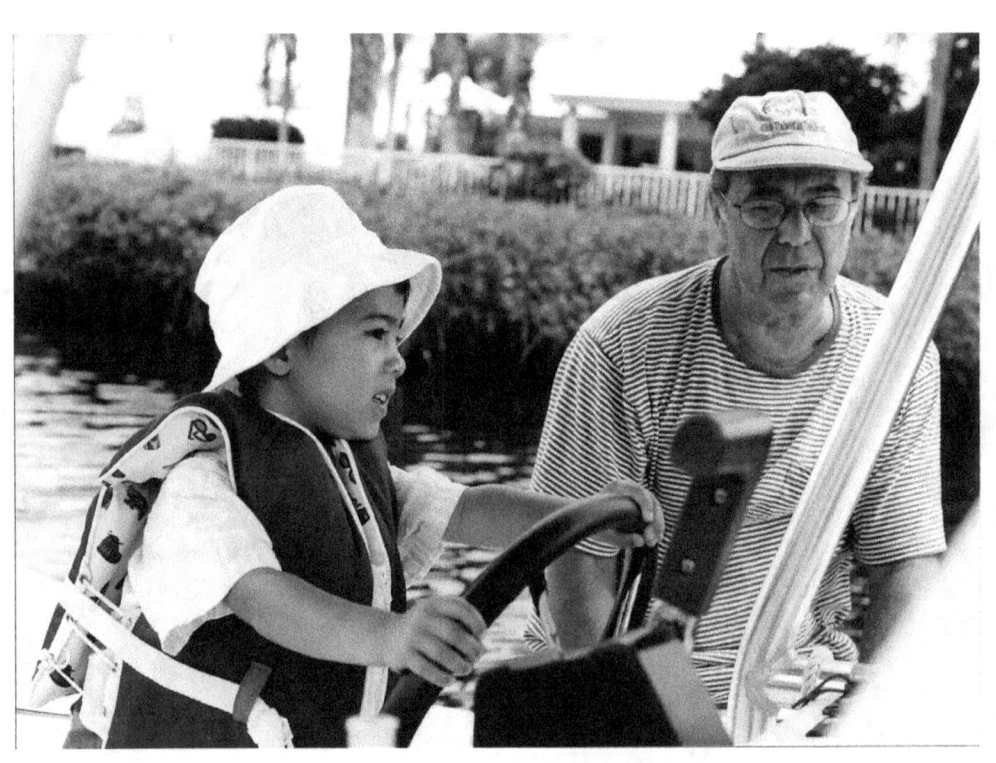

America

To want freedom
At the price of peace
Or to want peace
At the price of freedom?
My Mommy's father's country
Is grappling with this
Right now.
Me?
All I think about
Is going at top speed.

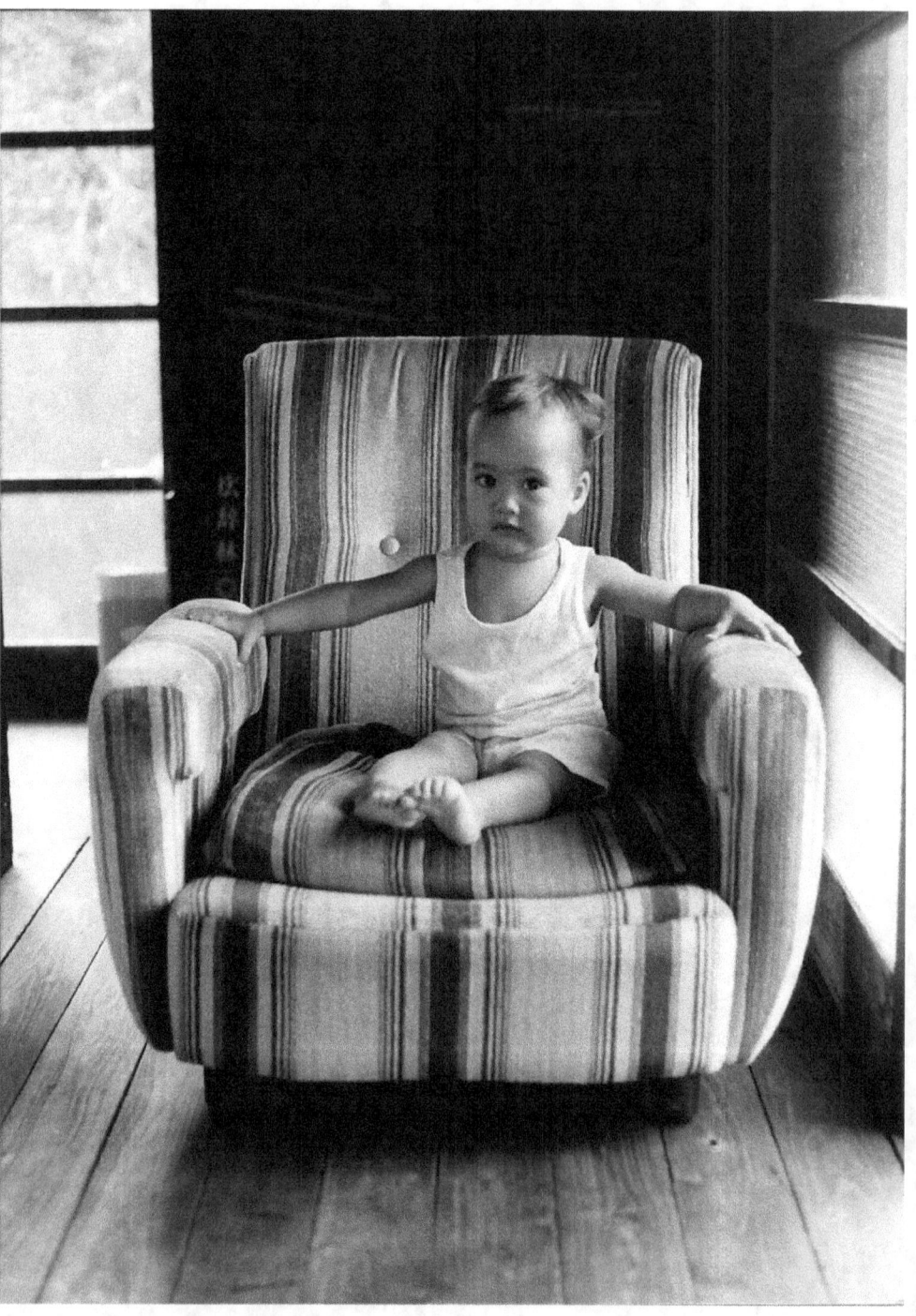

<u>Elegance</u>

Maya
Is sometimes
Scarily grown-up.
I don't know
If that is
Good or bad…

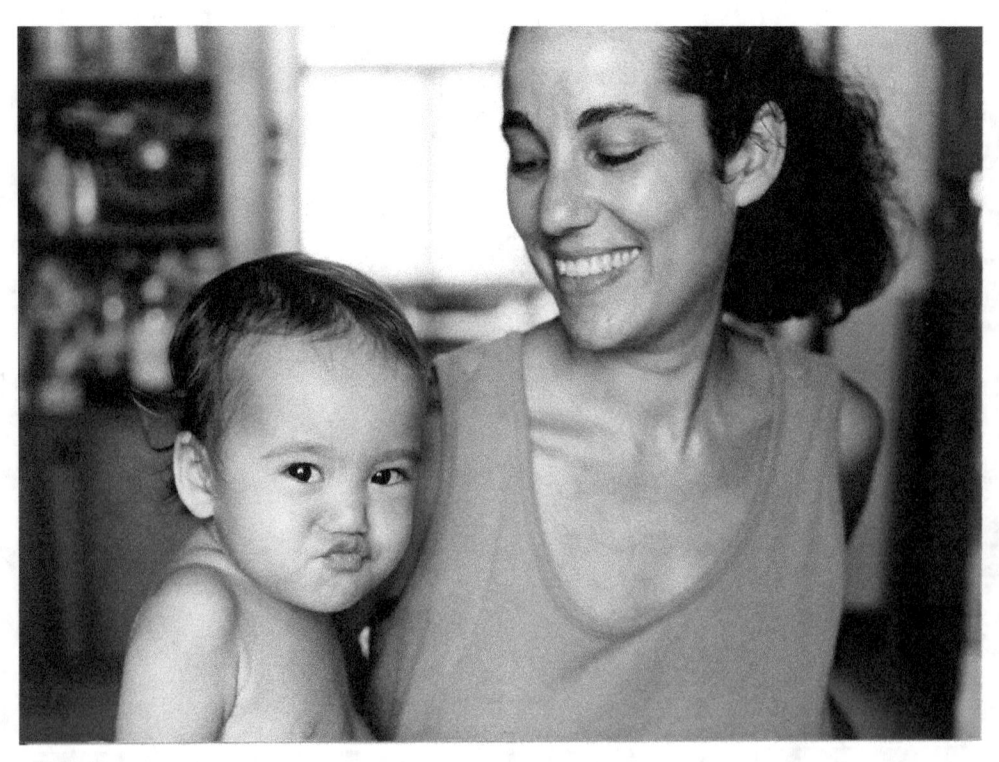

Happiness

When my Mommy laughs
It makes me happy.
Then Maya starts to giggle, too.
Which makes me even happier.
If this continues
More and more
Things can only get
Better and better.

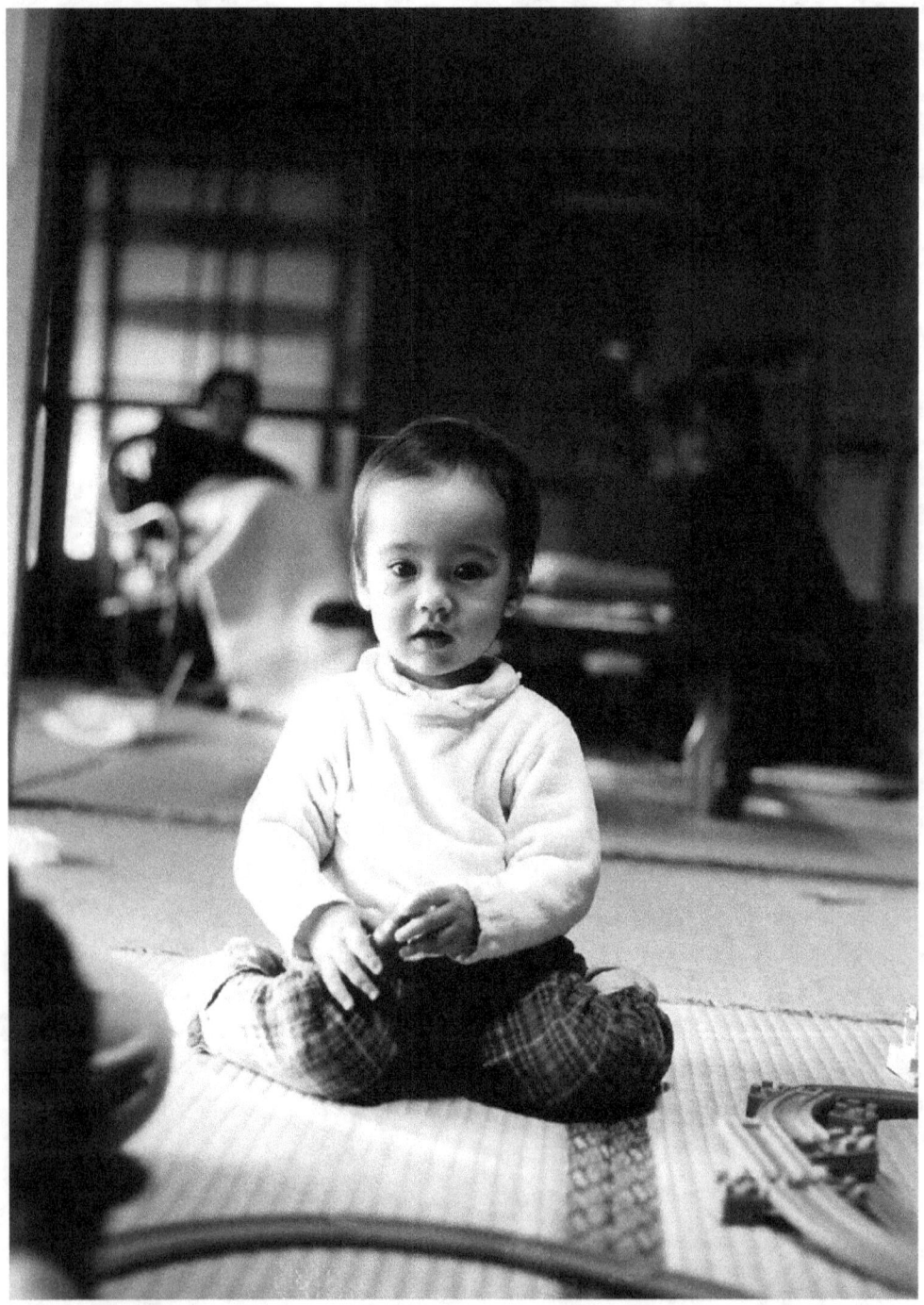

Carefree

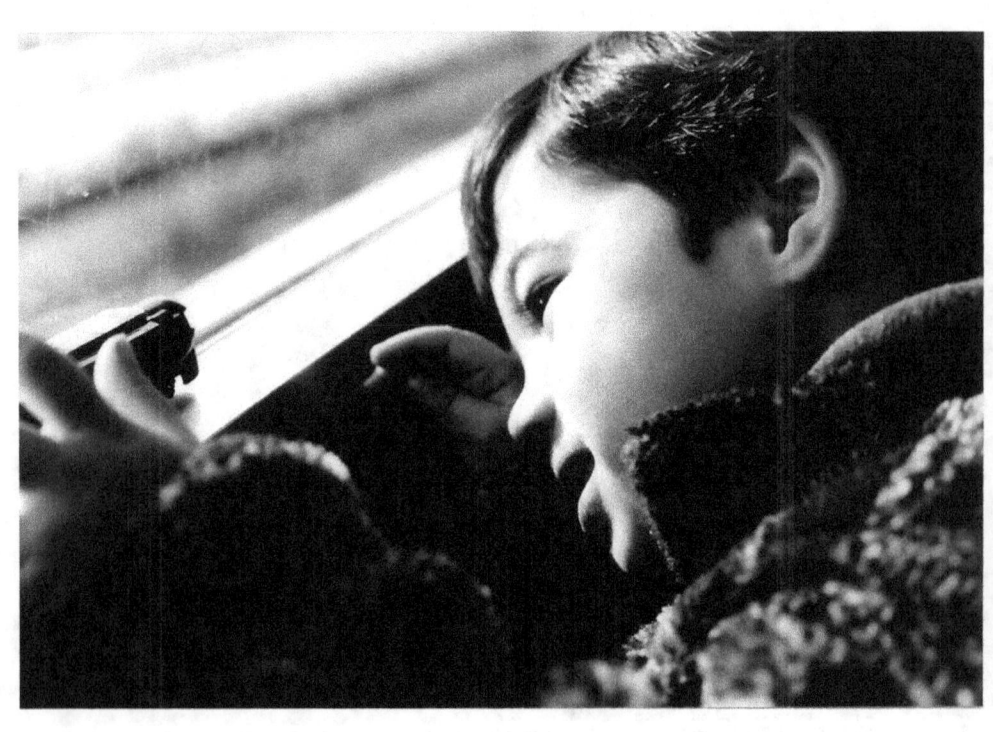

Life Size
To be oneself.
That means,
I can be ALL of myself

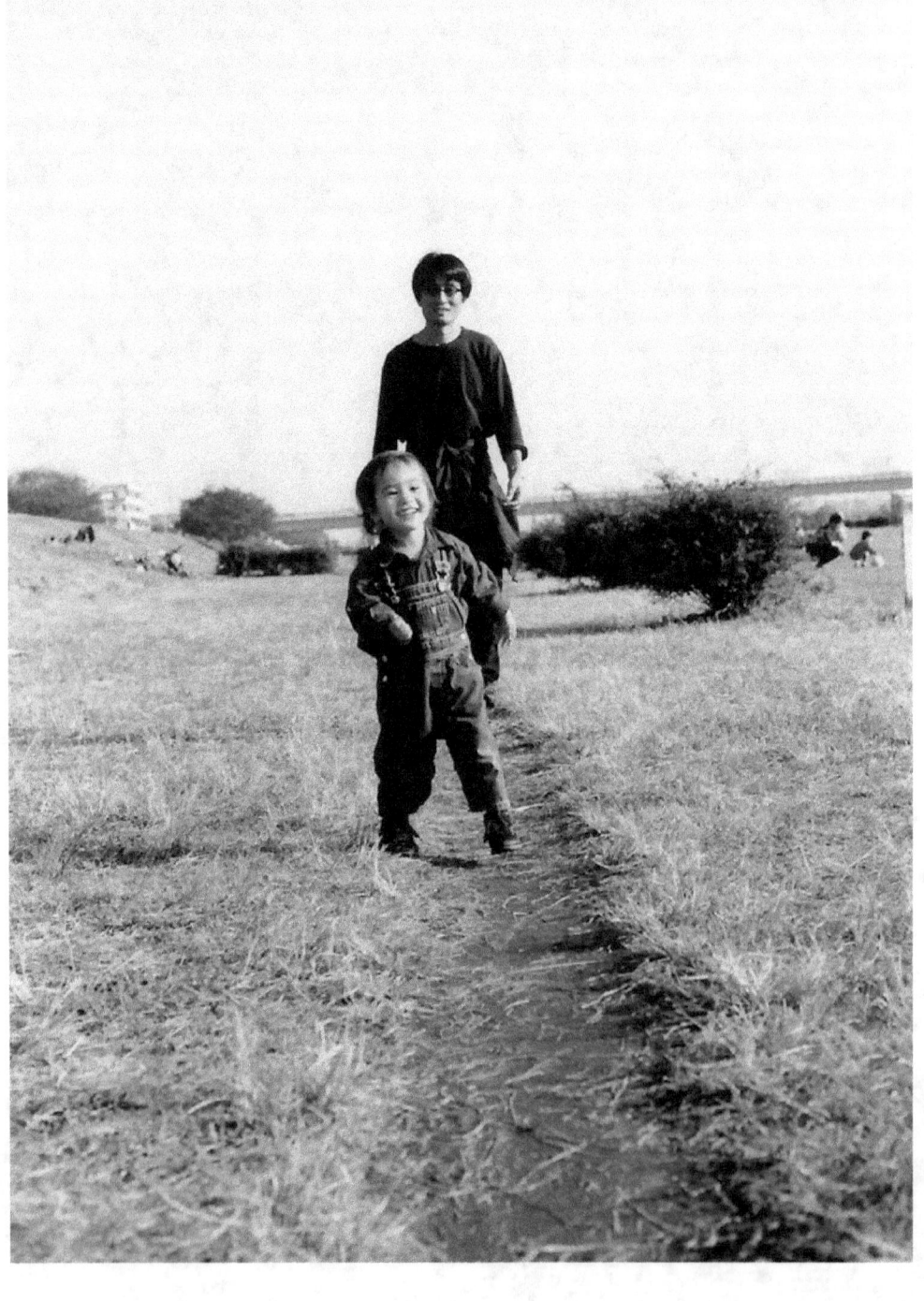

Keep an Eye on Her

What? Where?
Before we knew it
Maya wasn't there.
The park on the exposed riverbed of the Tama River.
It was the day of our Field Day event.
Mommy and Daddy ran helter skelter.
After all, it's right next to the river.
Of course, they ran around shouting,
"Maya! Where are you?"
Maya was nearby
Walking along the bank
Humming to herself.
Maya is always humming to herself.
Spritely, steadily, alone, walking.
Which is why we must always keep an eye on her
Where is she headed?
What kind of sister will she become?

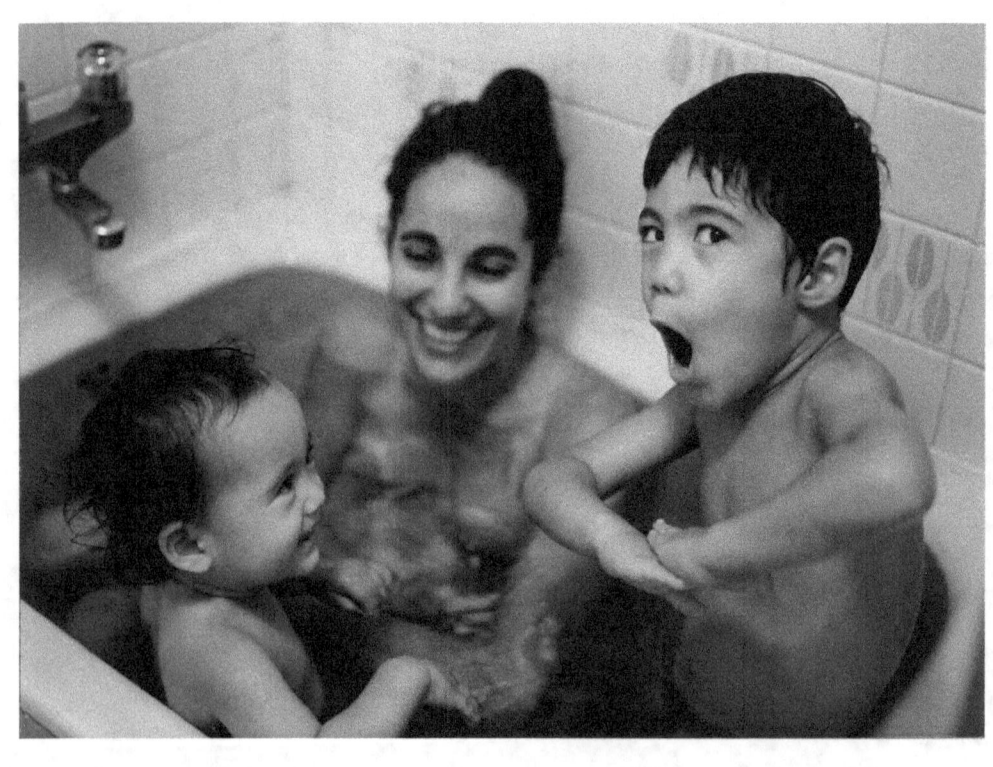

Family

Families are sometimes annoying.
My Mommy just about faints
Whenever she sees a spider.
My Daddy is terrified
Of fish eyes.
Me?
Well, once I stuffed my pocket with 20 roly polies.
The only laid back one is Maya.
She's not afraid of anything.
She'll touch anything.

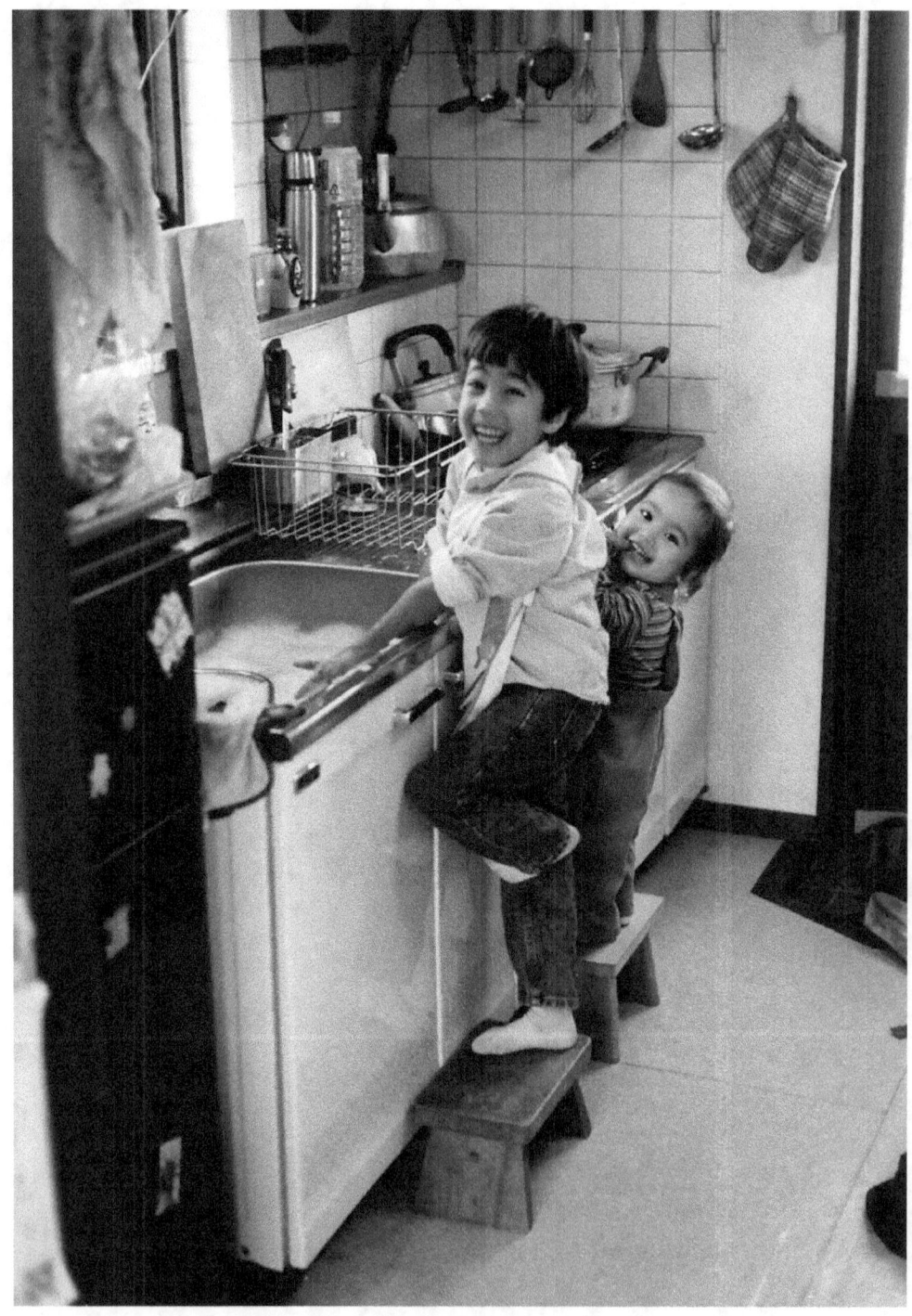

The Two of Us
There's no comparison.
Two is better than one.
I know from experience.
There's no mistaking it.
But,
Maybe 3 is better than 2?
I have no way of knowing.

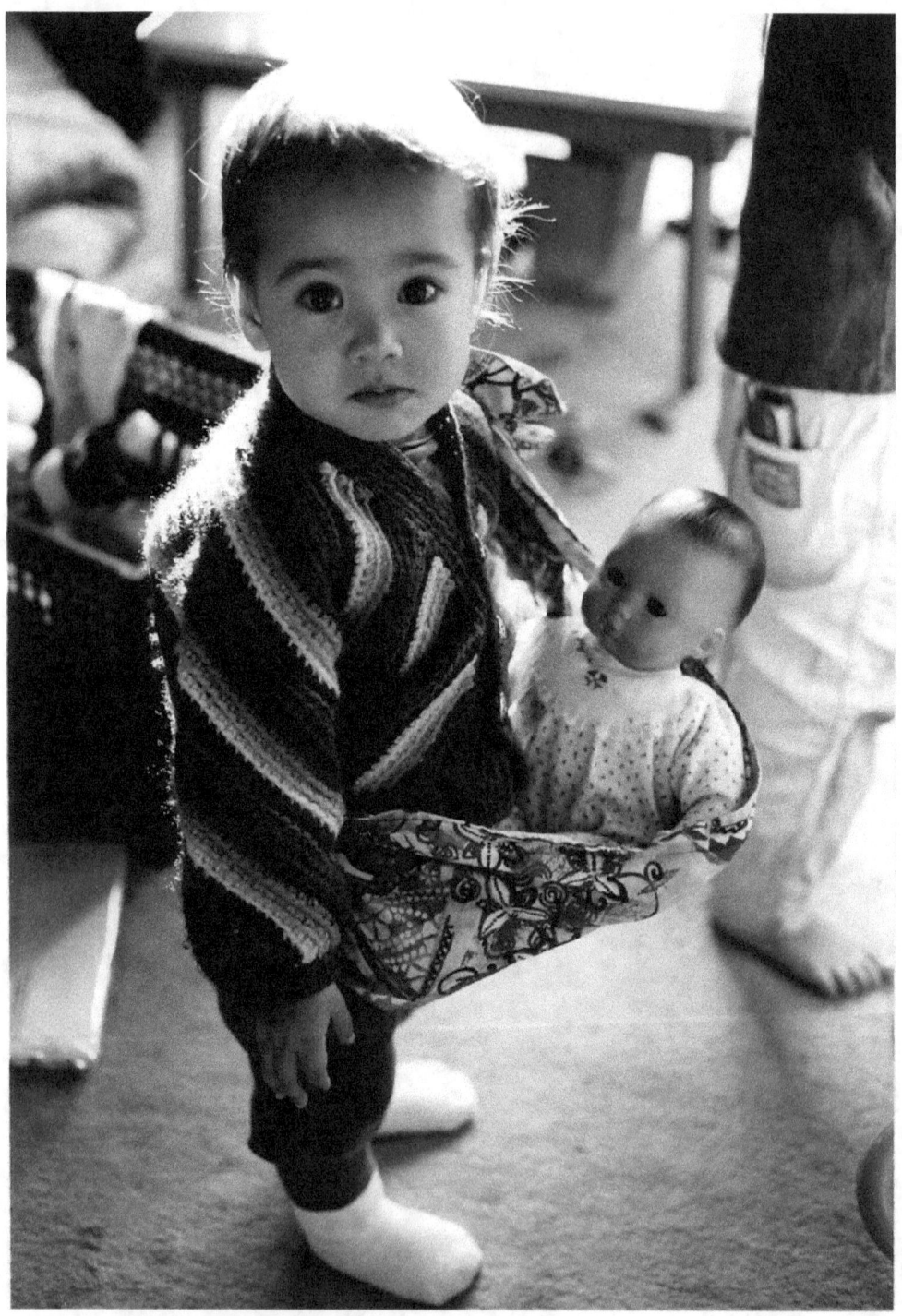

Maternal Instinct? Child Instinct?

Maya is adorable,

Kind,

Charming, free,

Adventurous,

Well-mannered.

On top of that,

She's very energetic.

And she is filled with extraordinary curiosity.

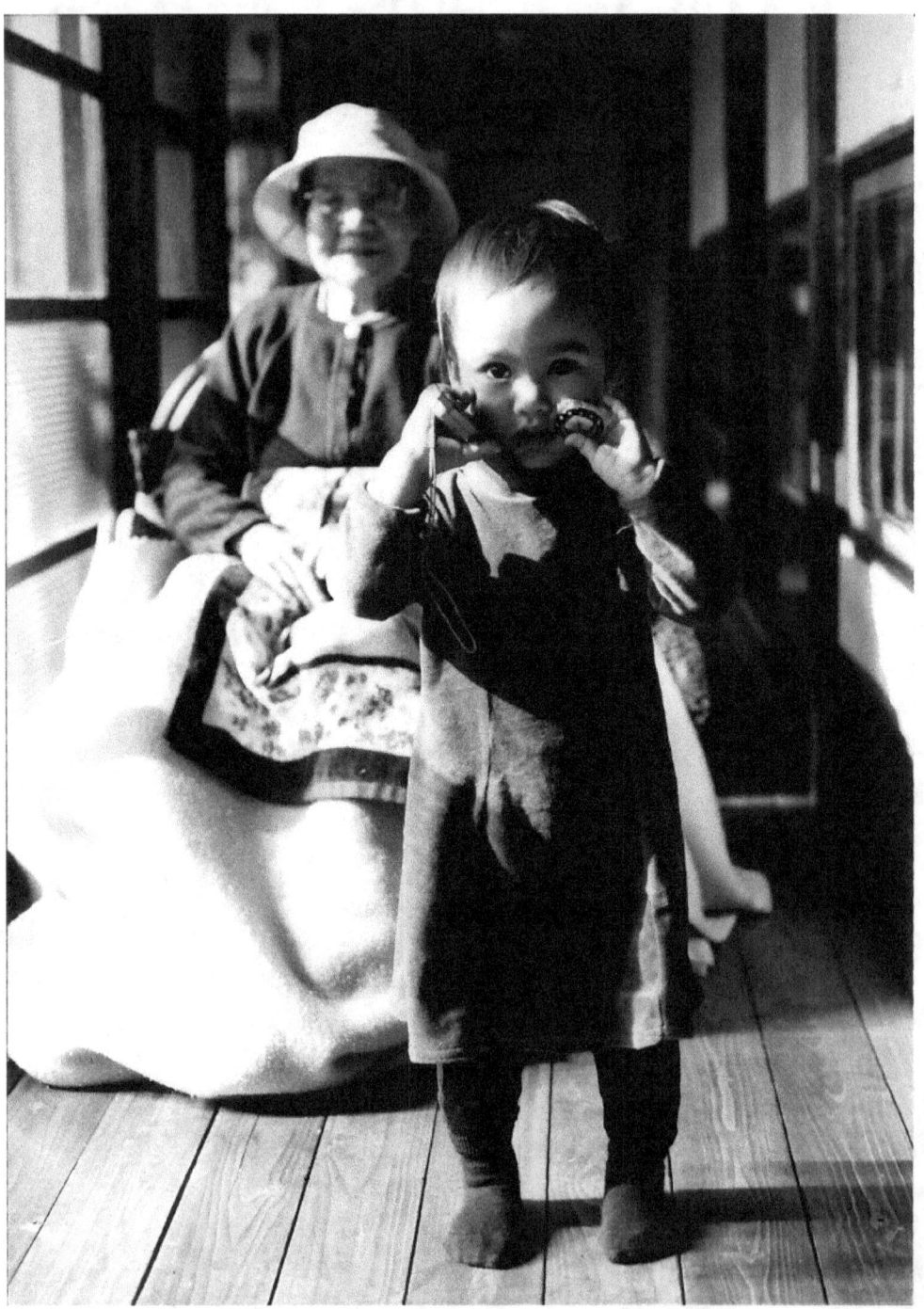

94 vs.1

*"Everyone is born
with a certain amount.
I've just about used up mine."
My Great-Grandmother, age 94.*

*Maya, age 1:
I think I get it.
To live life to the fullest
Must be awfully hard
But awfully important.*

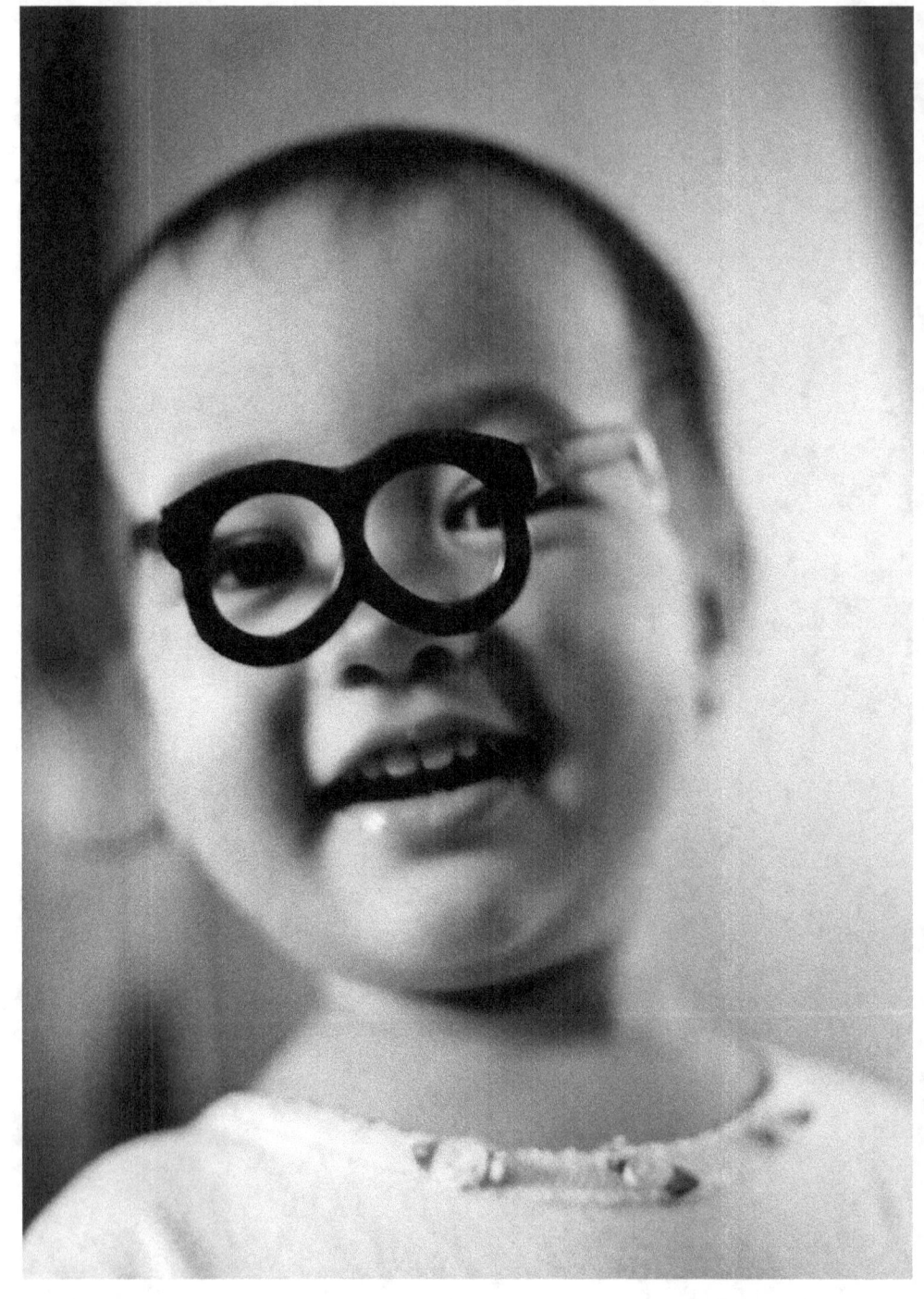

Look At Me!
Look!
Look!
Were you looking?
Look!
Look!
Are you looking?
Maya's favorite phrase.

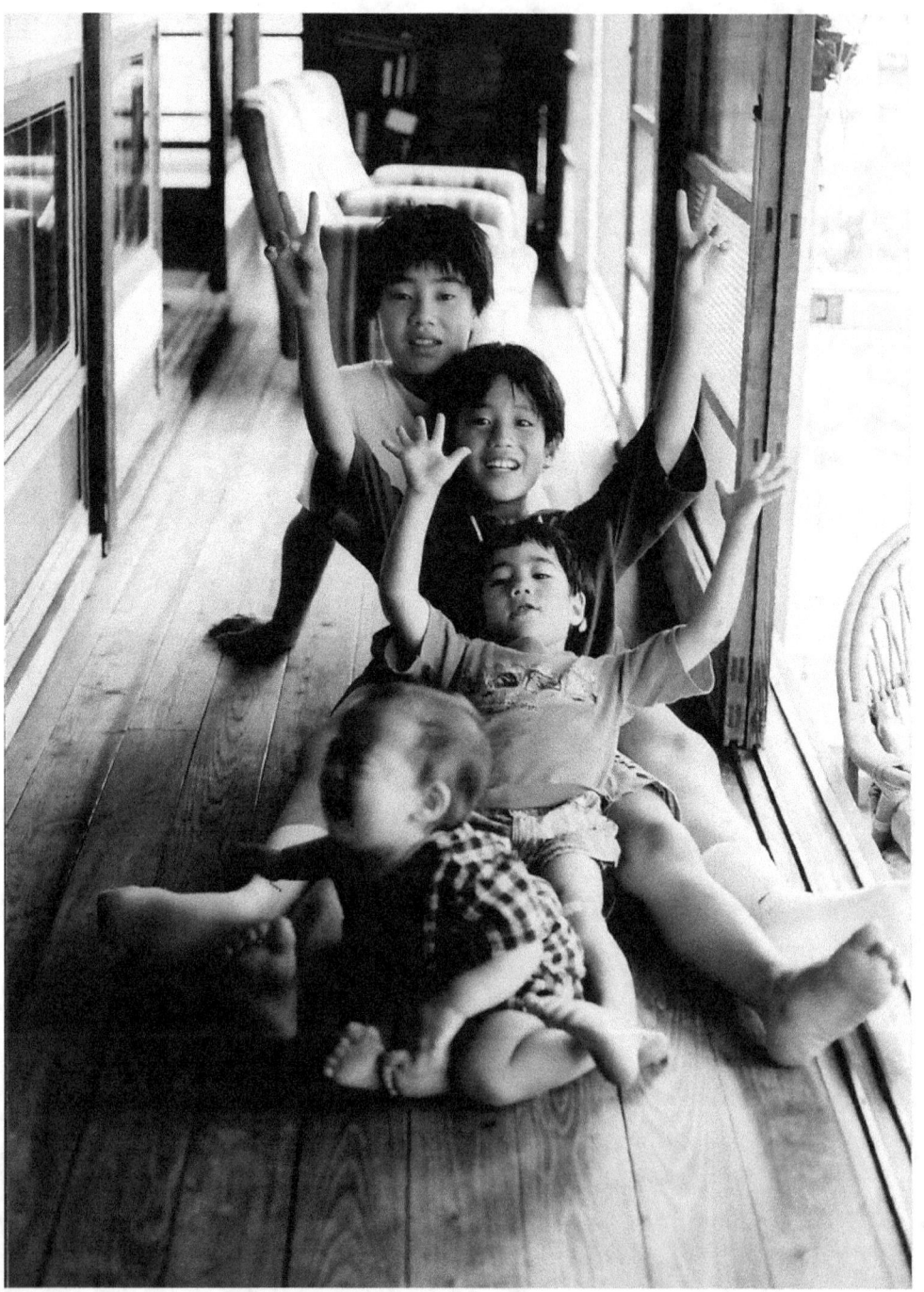

Cousins

Yuu and Jun are my
Daddy's older brother's children.
Maya and I are Yuu and Jun's Daddy's
Younger brother's children.
Hmmm...
But saying that leaves out Mommy.
What should I do? Maya!
Let's think about that together.

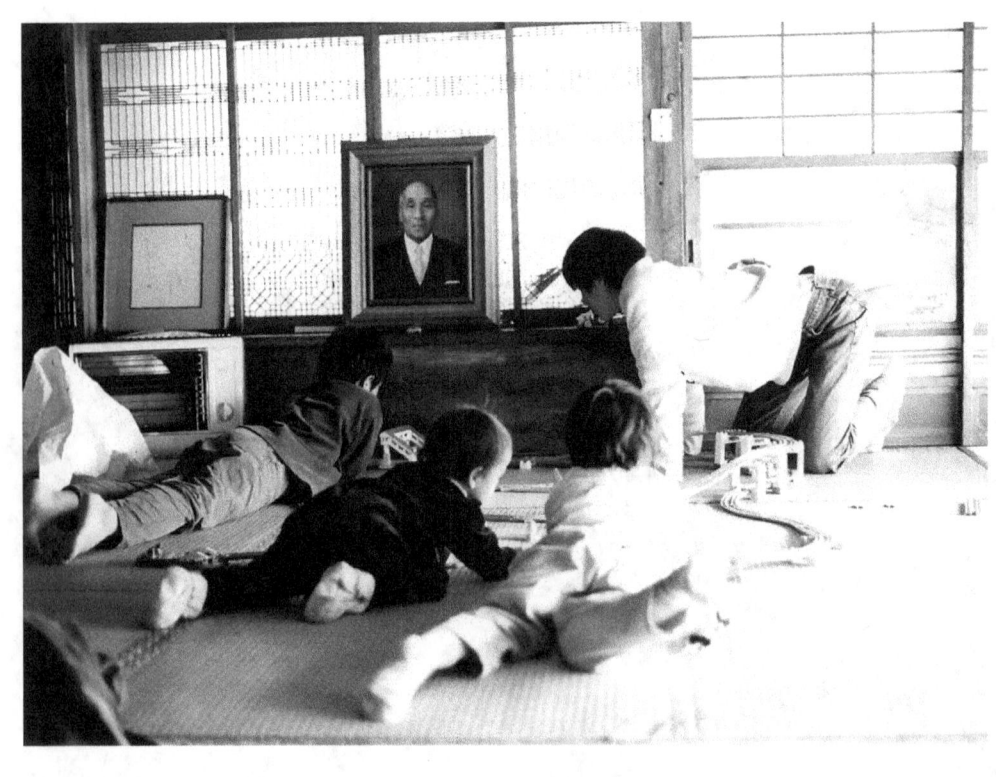

A Conversation With My Great-Grandfather

What's it like to die?

Does it hurt?

Is it painful?

Is it cold?

If you don't want to, do you have to?

Does everyone die?

When?

Where?

Noa and Maya, too?

Great Grandpa, too?

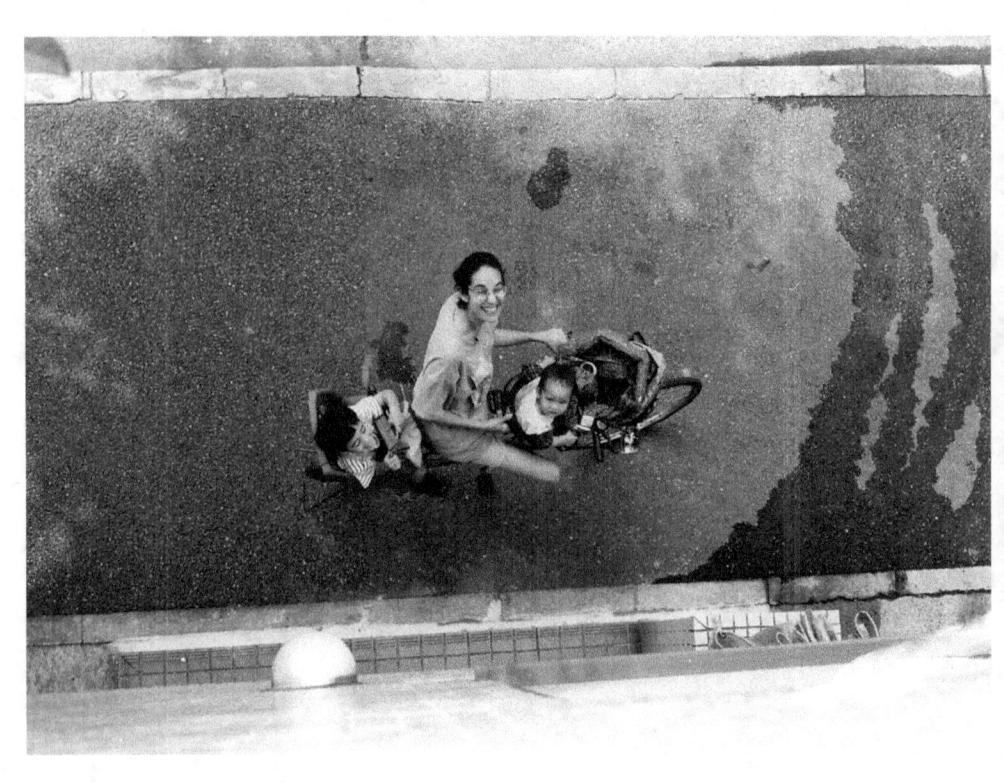

Mommy's bicycle
We go everywhere on Mommy's bicycle!

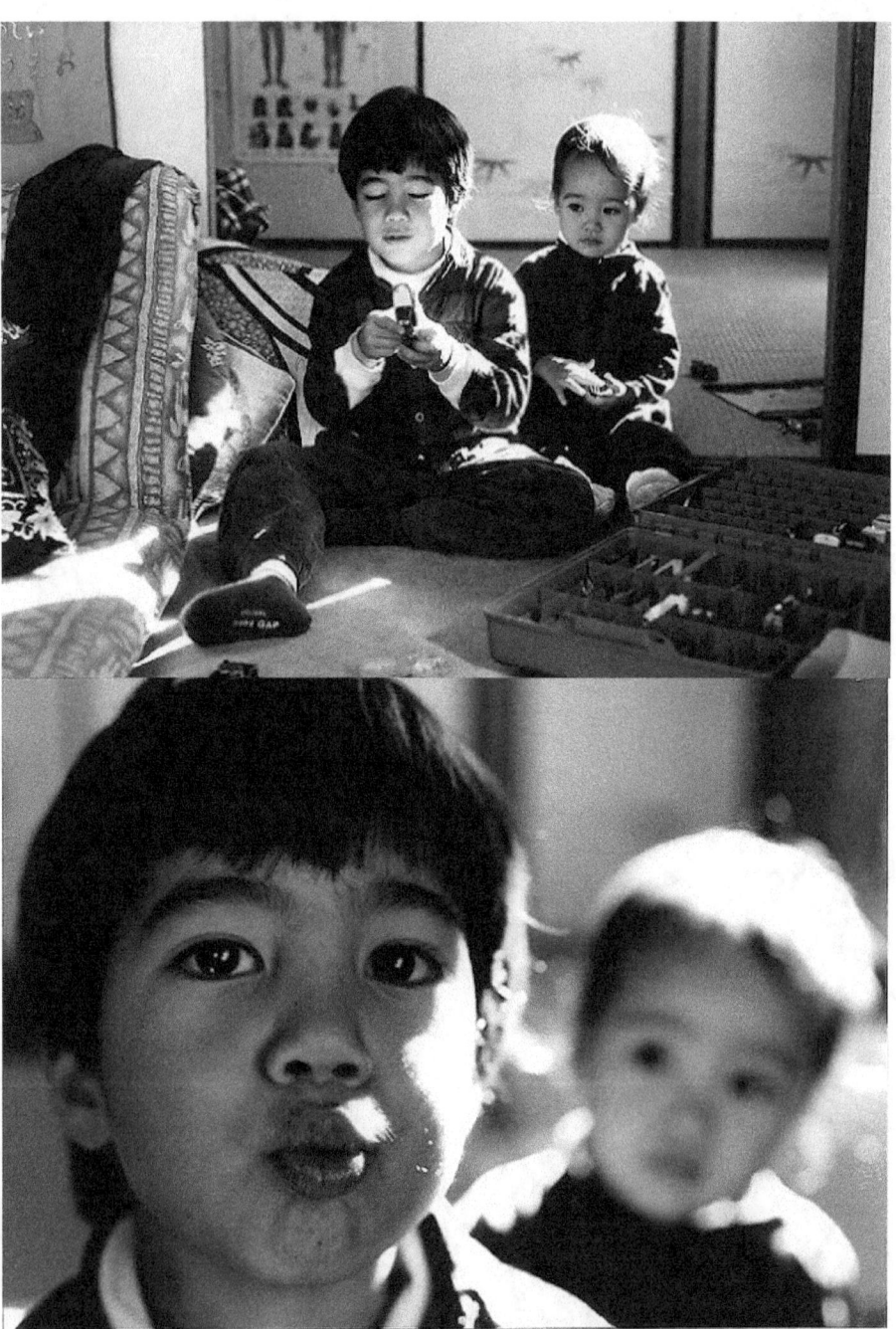

The Age of The Child
My Daddy says,
"Have courage to confront whatever lies ahead,
to conquer your fears.
If obstacles arise, pay them no heed,
Throw them aside."
I ask him why.
He looks at me sadly.
"Right now is when you, Noa,
Are at your most vulnerable, you have the most to lose,
Because you are alive."
I think I better
Go tell Maya about this, too.

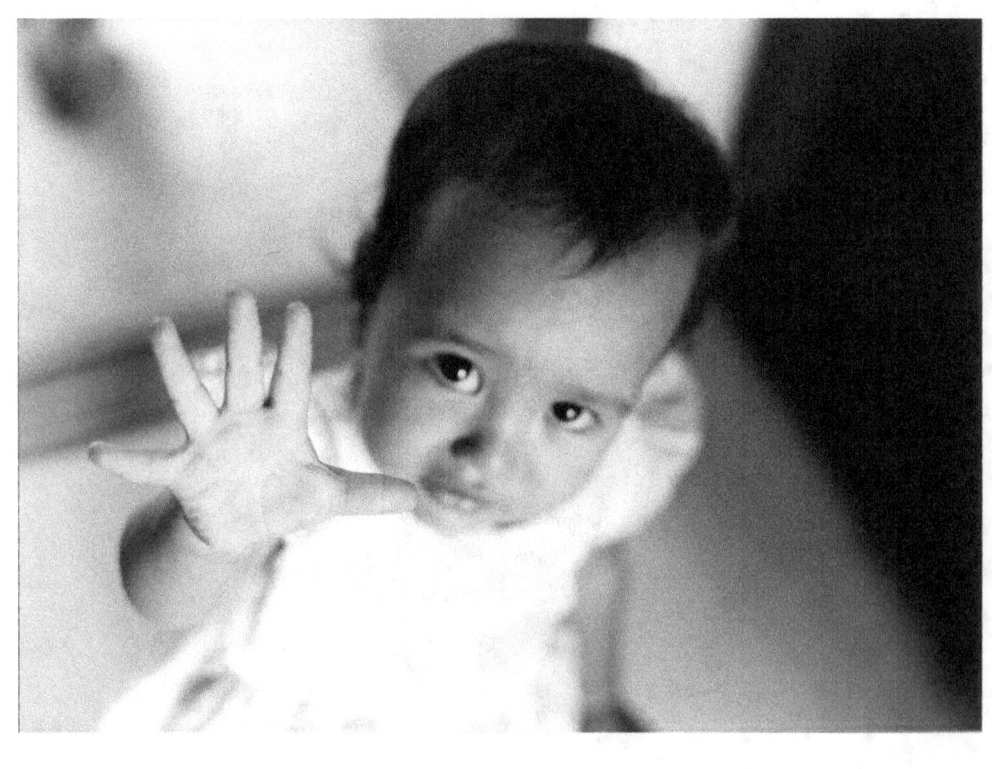

Really Weird

Why do children kill their Mommies and Daddies?
Why do Mommies and Daddies kill their children?
That is really weird.
How do they come to feel that way?
How do they become such a person?
Don't they remember when they were little?
Don't they ask their parents about when they were young?
We were all vulnerable once.
Weren't we all pure, too?
Let's all try to remember when we had the heart and mind of a newborn.
Our hands were so small.
Do you think a knife looks becoming in that hand?

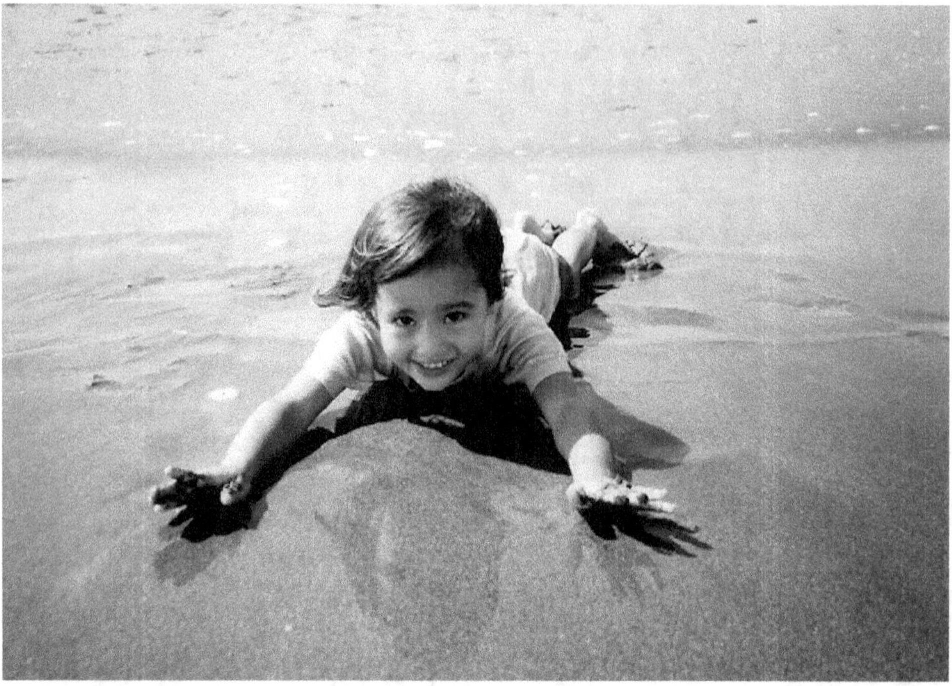

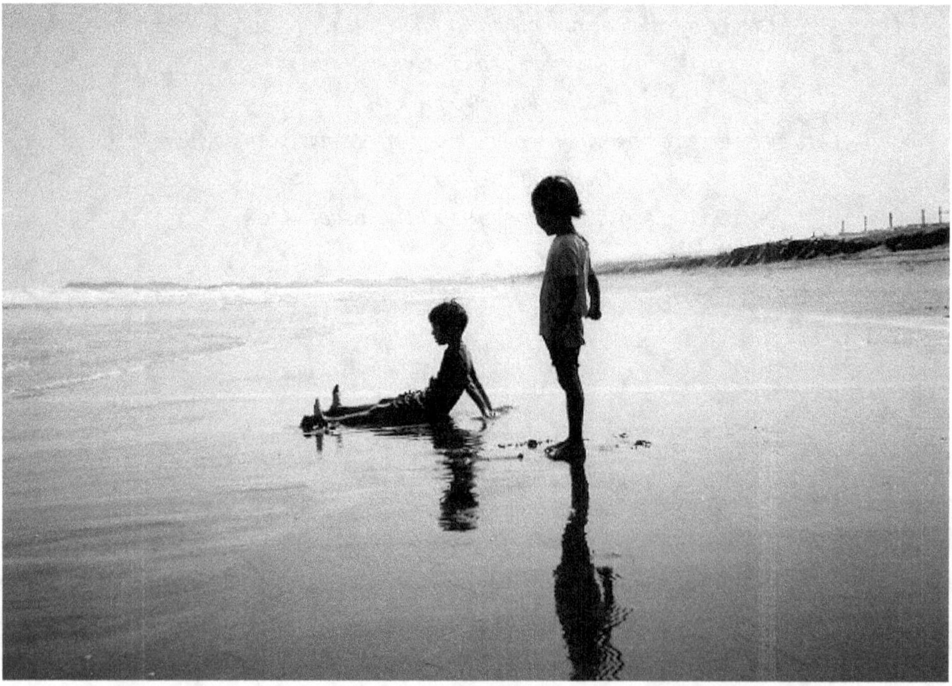

At the Ocean

The ocean is so warm.

Water – it feels so good.

So calm, so rich, not a worry in the world.

The ocean is strong and can put up with a lot.

Did you know?

Whales hear "Earth sounds" and can use telepathy.

"Earth sounds" carry the history of everything.

That's why whales can travel the whole ocean and never get lost.

Don't you think that's amazing?

Pretty nifty.

That's why we can NEVER pollute the oceans.

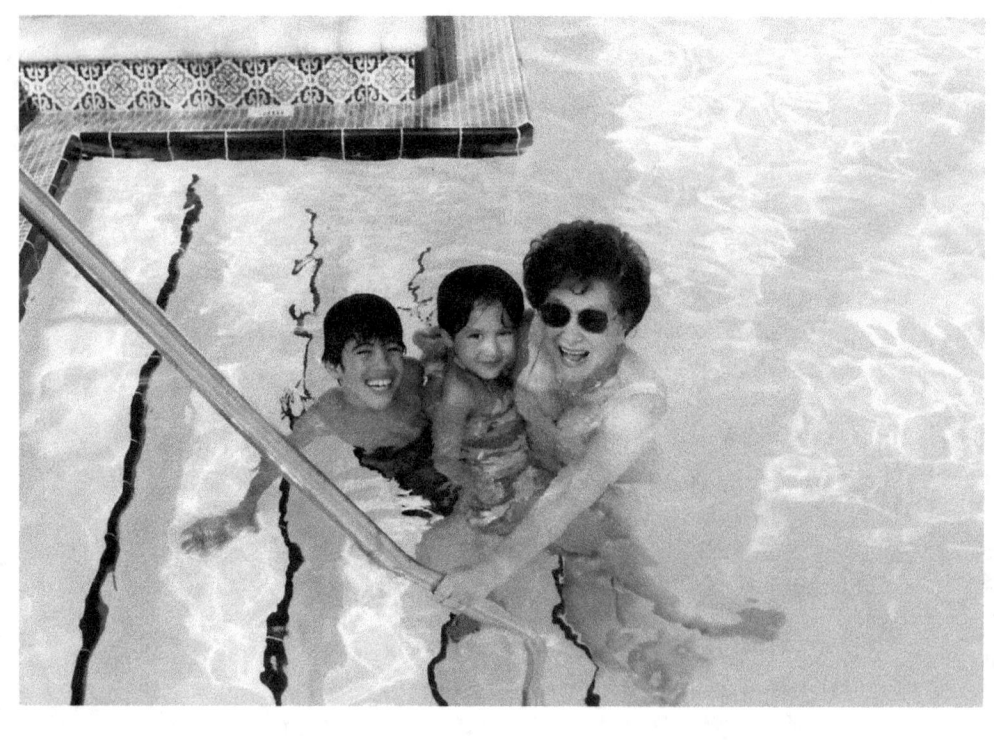

In Florida

Sunglasses suit her.
My great-grandmother who lives in Florida.
"Great-grandmother" doesn't suit her.
In America,
grandmas are sometimes called "Nana."
Big-hearted, vivacious.
Good at cards.
If she played for real,
she'd probably win big all in one night.
I'm in the midst of special training in a game called canasta
So I can become Nana's best partner.

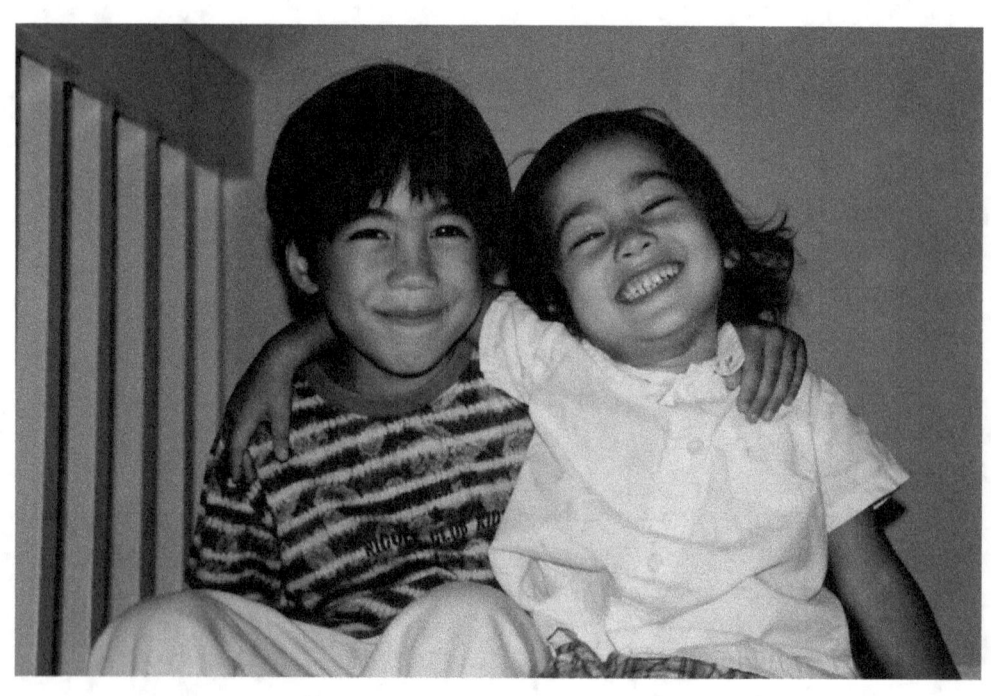

Crescent Moon Eyes

I wonder what this exhilarating feeling is…
Happiness?
Fun?
Funny?
I don't know but it's mine.
It's exhilarating.
My chest is squeezed with pleasure.
I really wonder what it is.

And then…

12 years later…

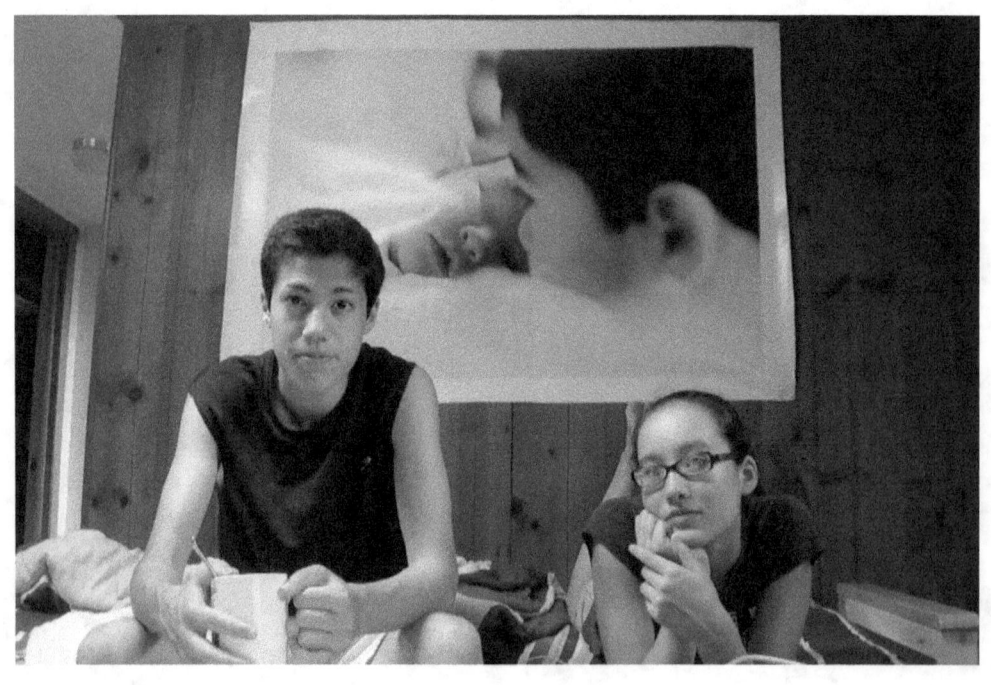

18 & 15

What has changed in the past 12 years?
Uncle Aki is gone,
Great Grandmother followed after Great Grandfather.
And then Sei-chan.
Grandma's mother, Nana, also died.
They were all such wonderful people.
They left me many memories.
It's said that humans are animals who forget.
Not us.

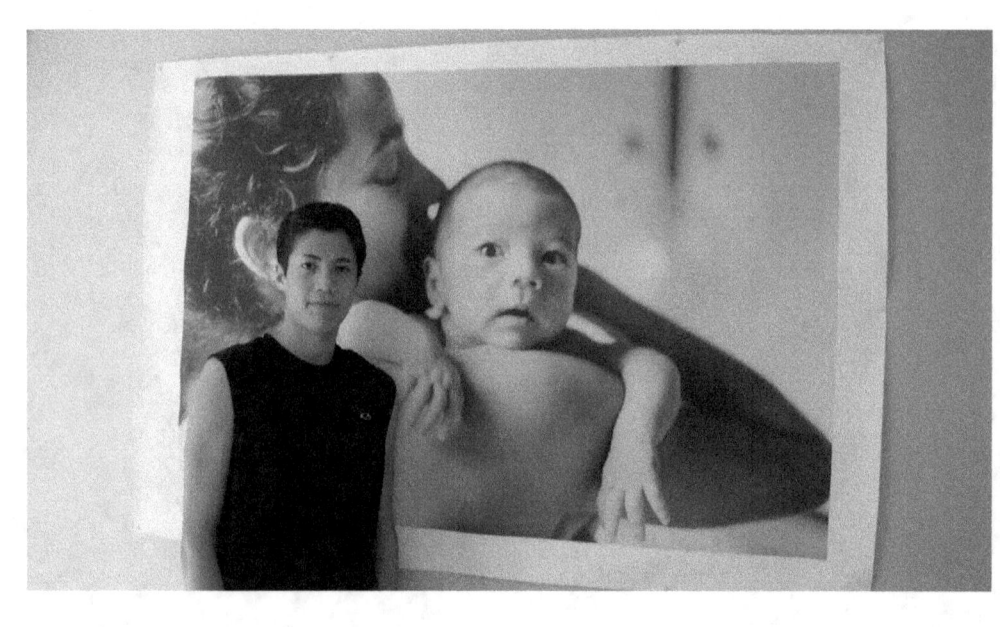

A frog? Well? I guess so...

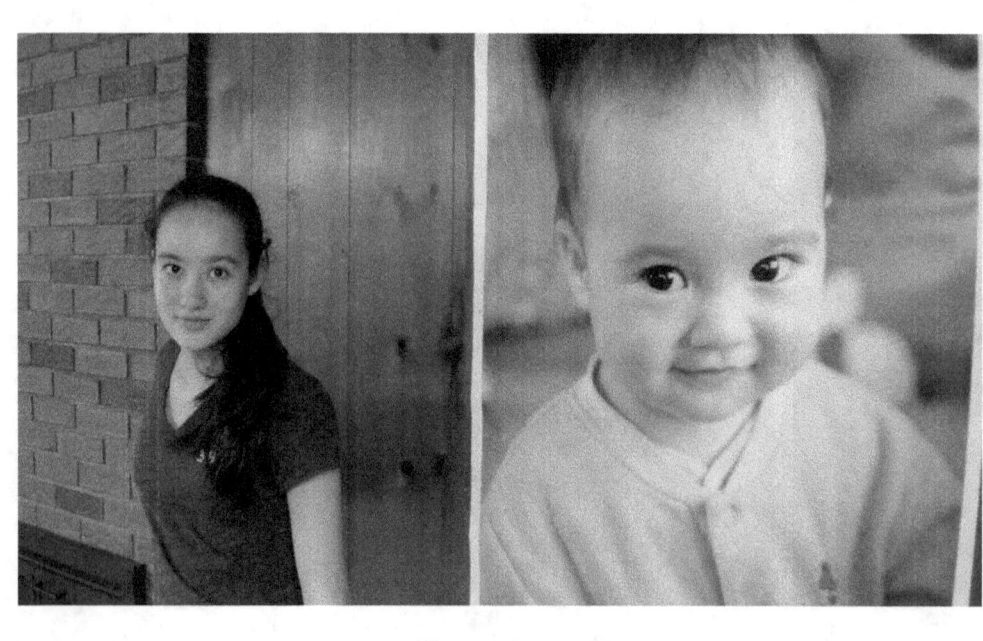

Forever Kewpie

According to Maya,
When she was young,
perhaps she was a Kewpie doll or a peanut or a baby Capybara.
What kind of an animal is a Capybara?

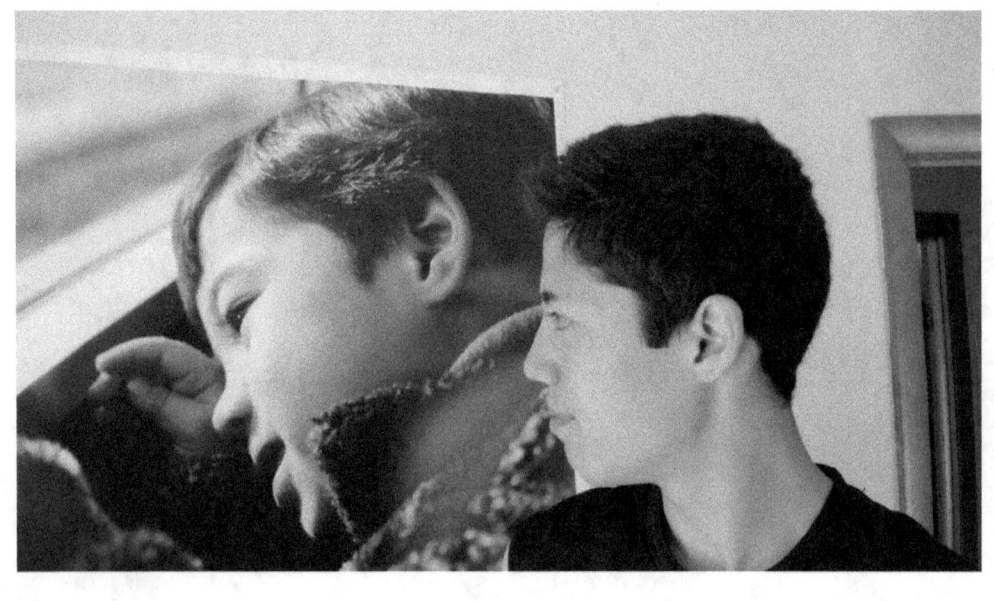

See any similarity?

Well, I suppose so, of course.

Yes, absolutely.

Slap dang.

You could roll me with a spoon.

Look alike?

Yeah, I guess so.

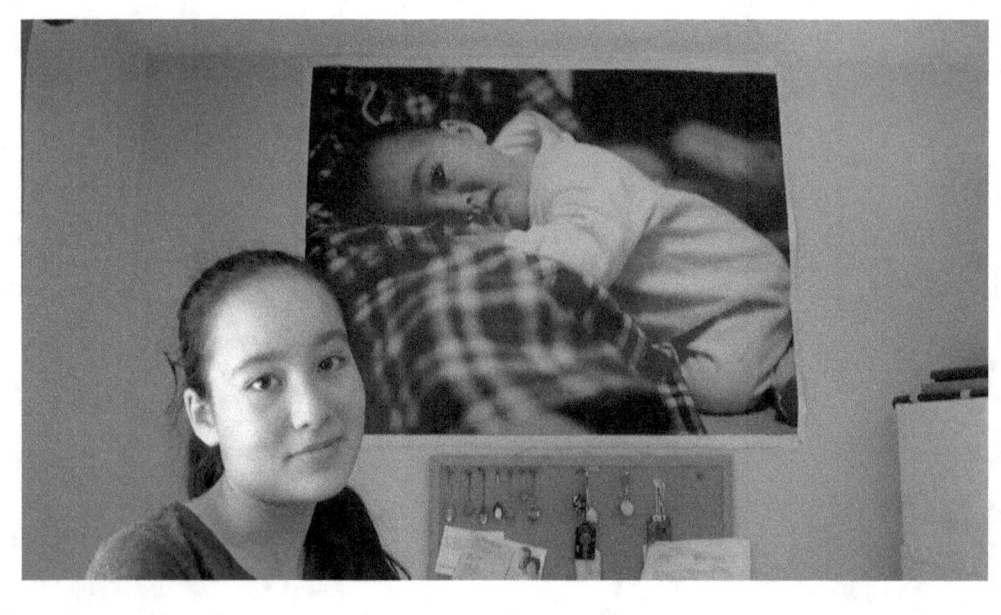

What was she thinking?
She must remember, I'm sure.

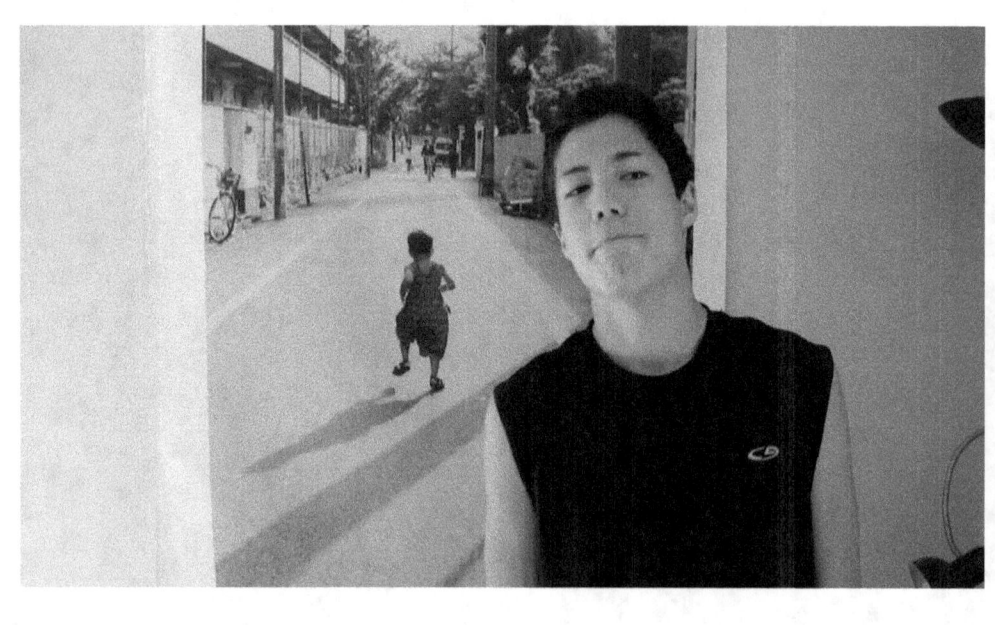

Still Running

Joined a soccer team in third grade,
from that point on, 'till now.
Am I still putting my all into it?
Of course.
Is there any other way of running?

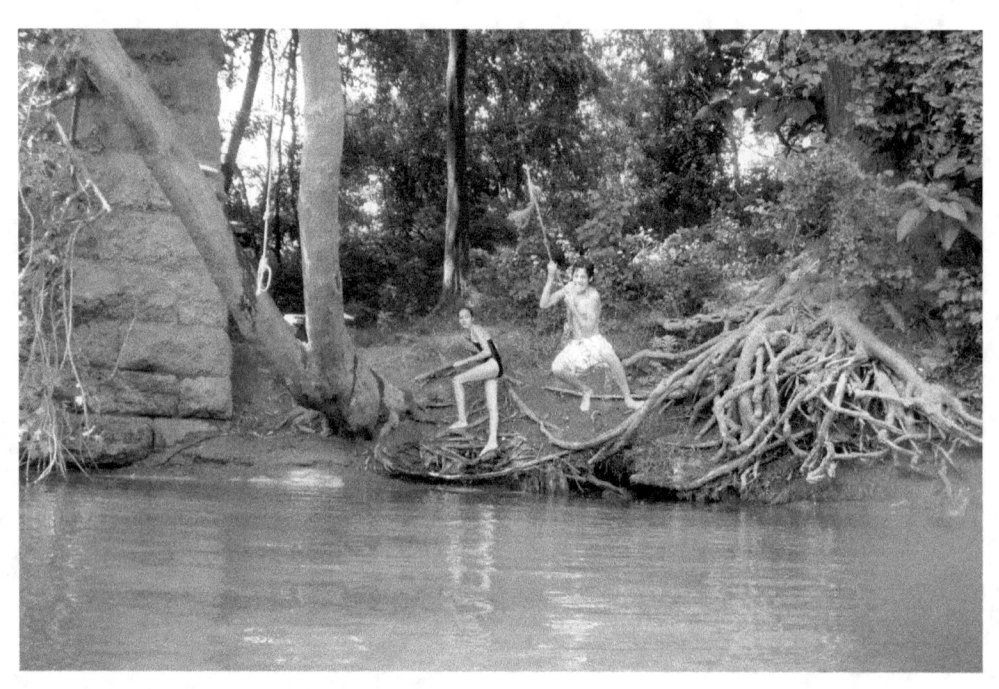

Summer

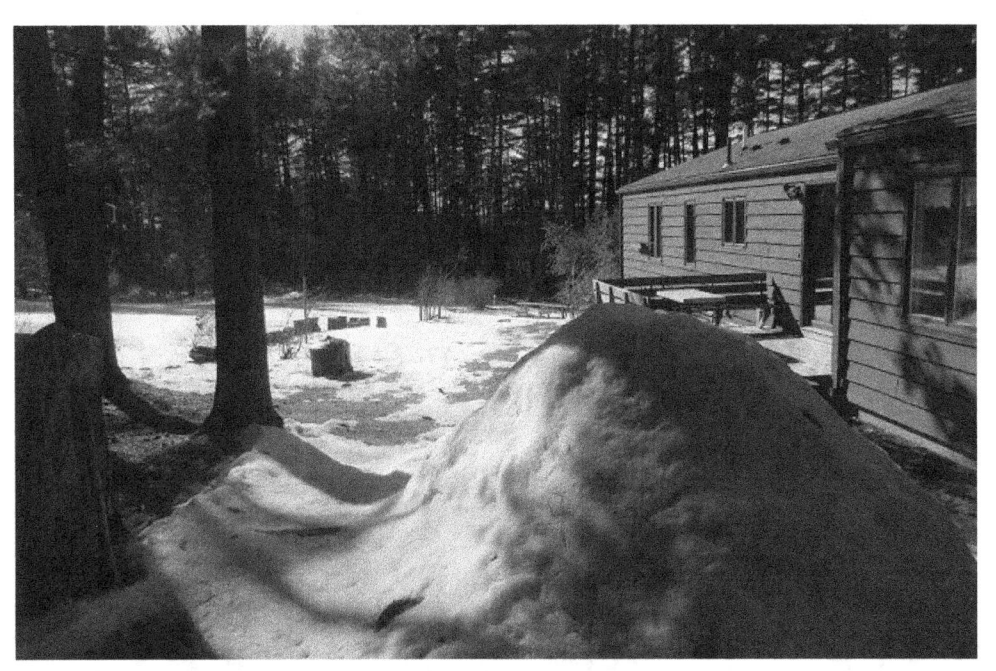

Winter

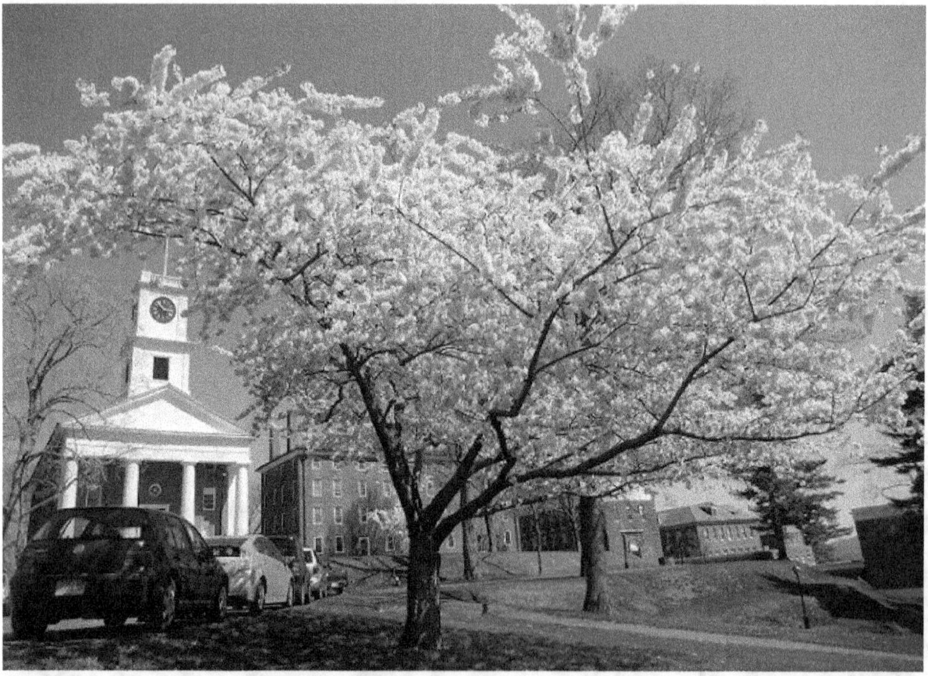

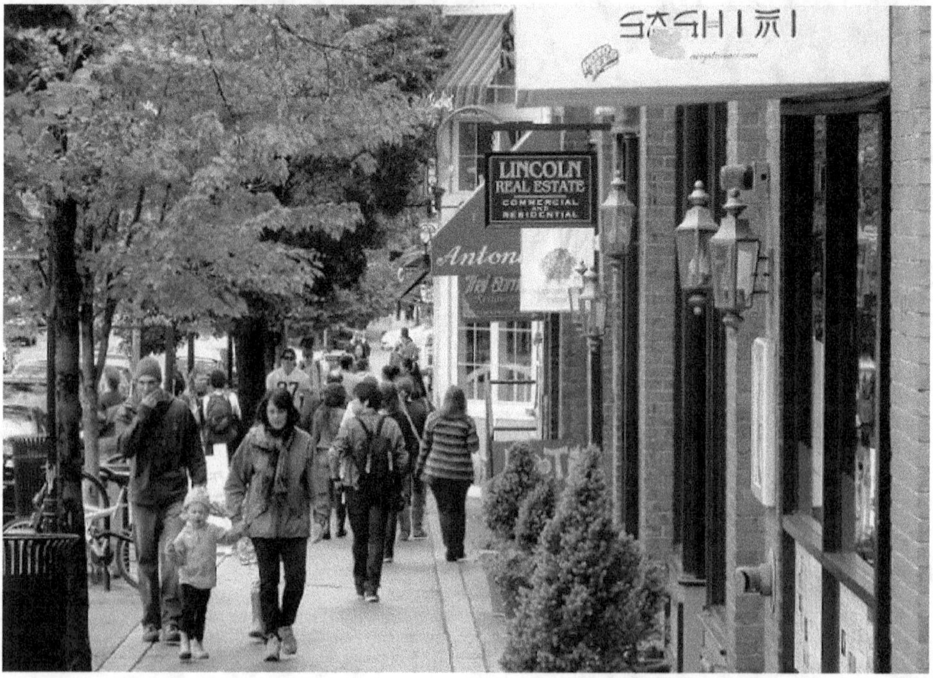

Our new habitat

Two years ago, we moved to America.

Amherst, Massachusetts.

Have you heard of it?

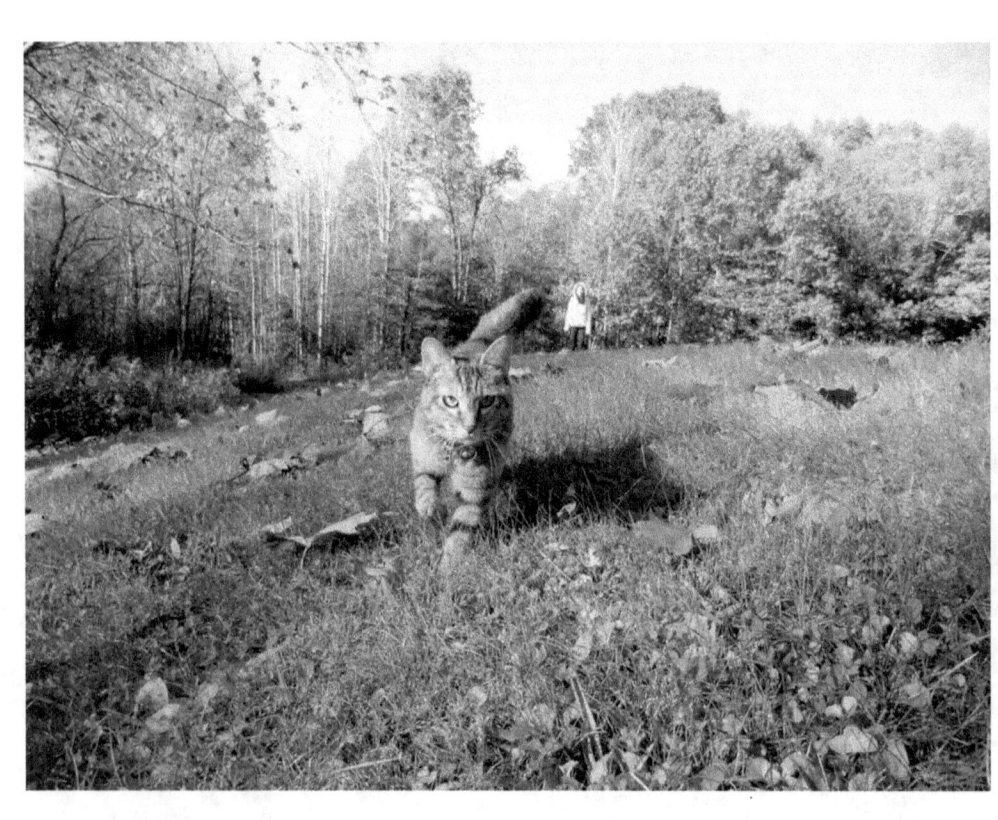

A Walk with Milky

Yes, Milky was a cat.

Eight years ago, someone left her in a box in the park.

She was tiny and her eyes were still closed.

She moved with us to America.

Unlike in Tokyo, she was free to roam the fields.

We'd go on walks together.

She'd even go fishing with me.

Can you believe that?

But last year, someone killed her.

The price of freedom?

Milky cannot be blamed one iota.

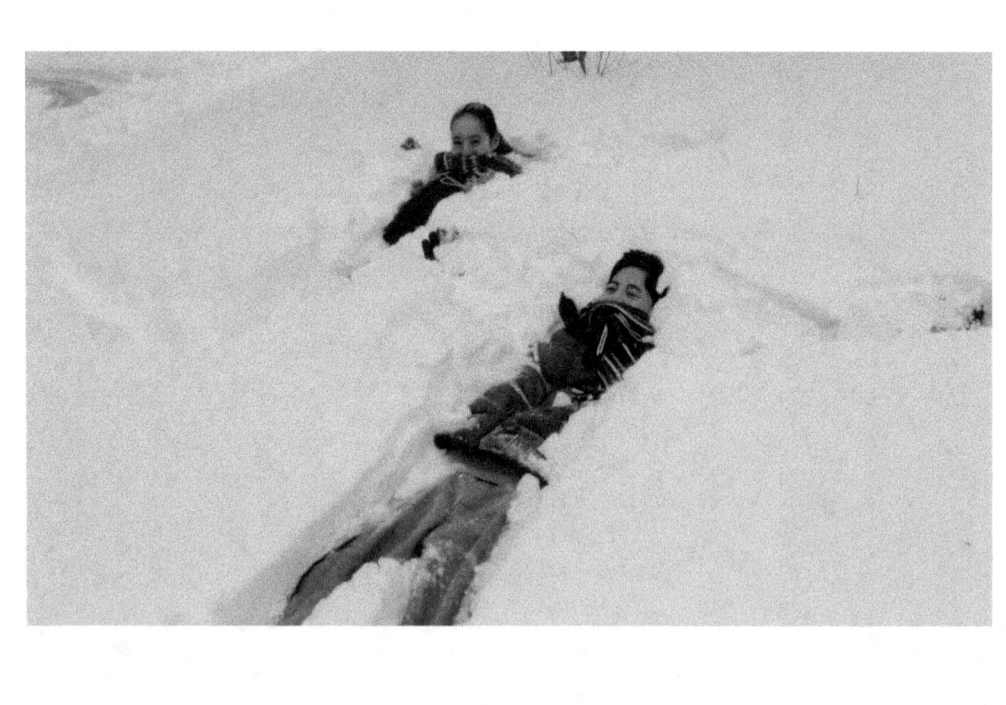

<u>In the Snow</u>

That

Was a terribly typical cold Massachusetts afternoon.

However, in the snow…

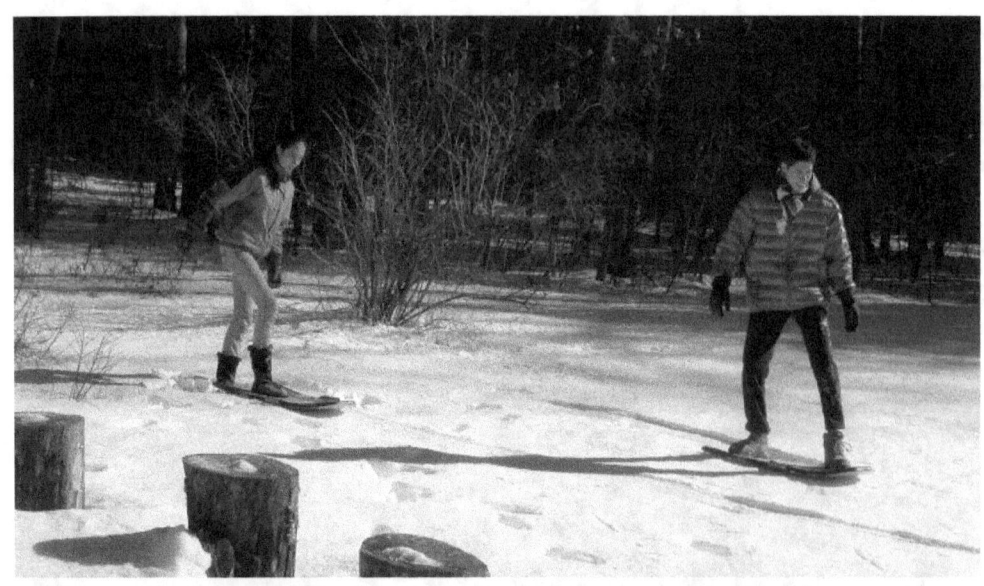

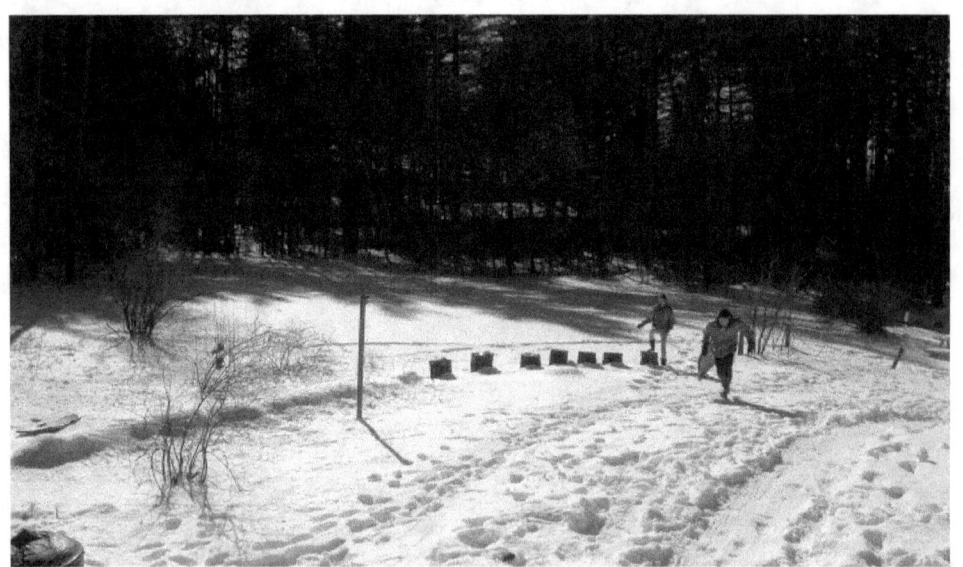

Reverting to the Mind of a Child?
You mean, I'm no longer a child?
But,
I awoke one morning to a silvery world outside my window.
I couldn't contain myself.
I'd like to hold onto this feeling forever.

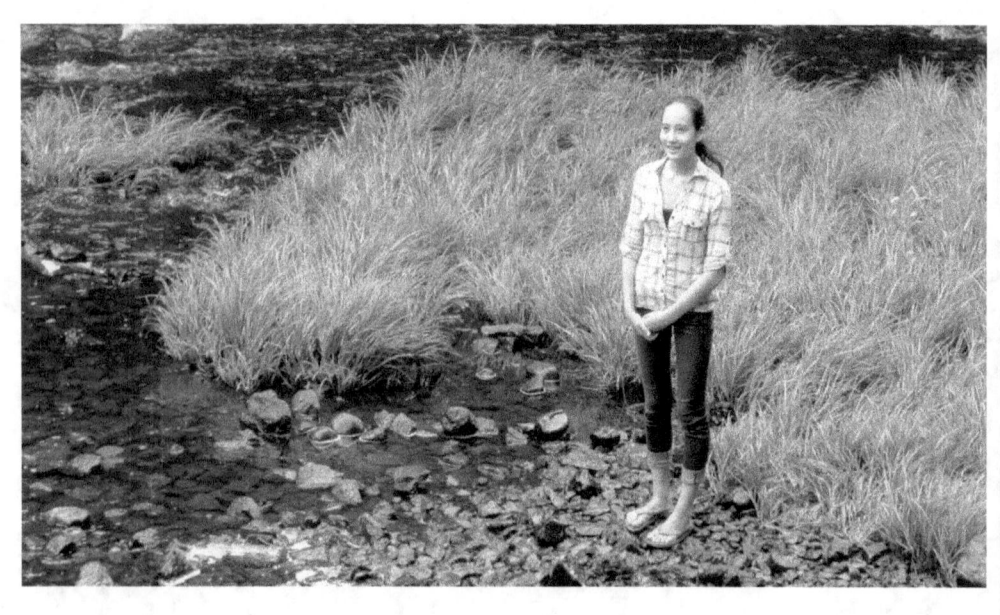

My How You've Grown…

You are already taller than Mom.
Dad wants you to hold on there just a minute.
So,
"Don't grow anymore!" has become his favorite refrain.
But that's a moot point.
What? Me?
Of course, I'm tallest by far – hehehe!
By the way, that Maya –
These past 7 years –
Sinewy from ballet.
She likes it so she improves; she improves so she likes it even more.
Just like when she was young: "More and more, better and better."

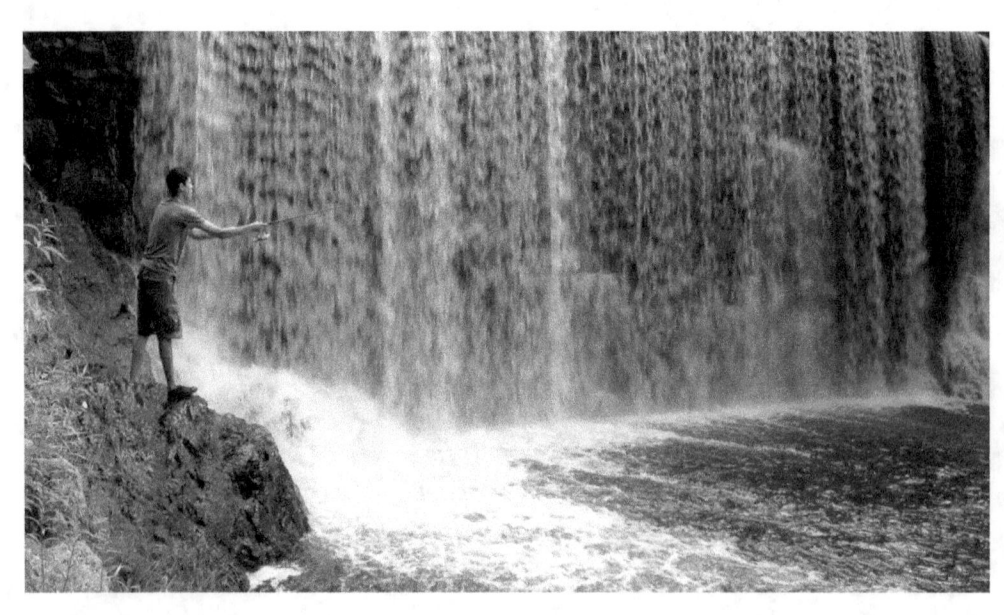

The Comfort Zone

It's important to find at least one such place.

"Noa, don't slip!"

"Don't worry. Watch out for your own two feet!"

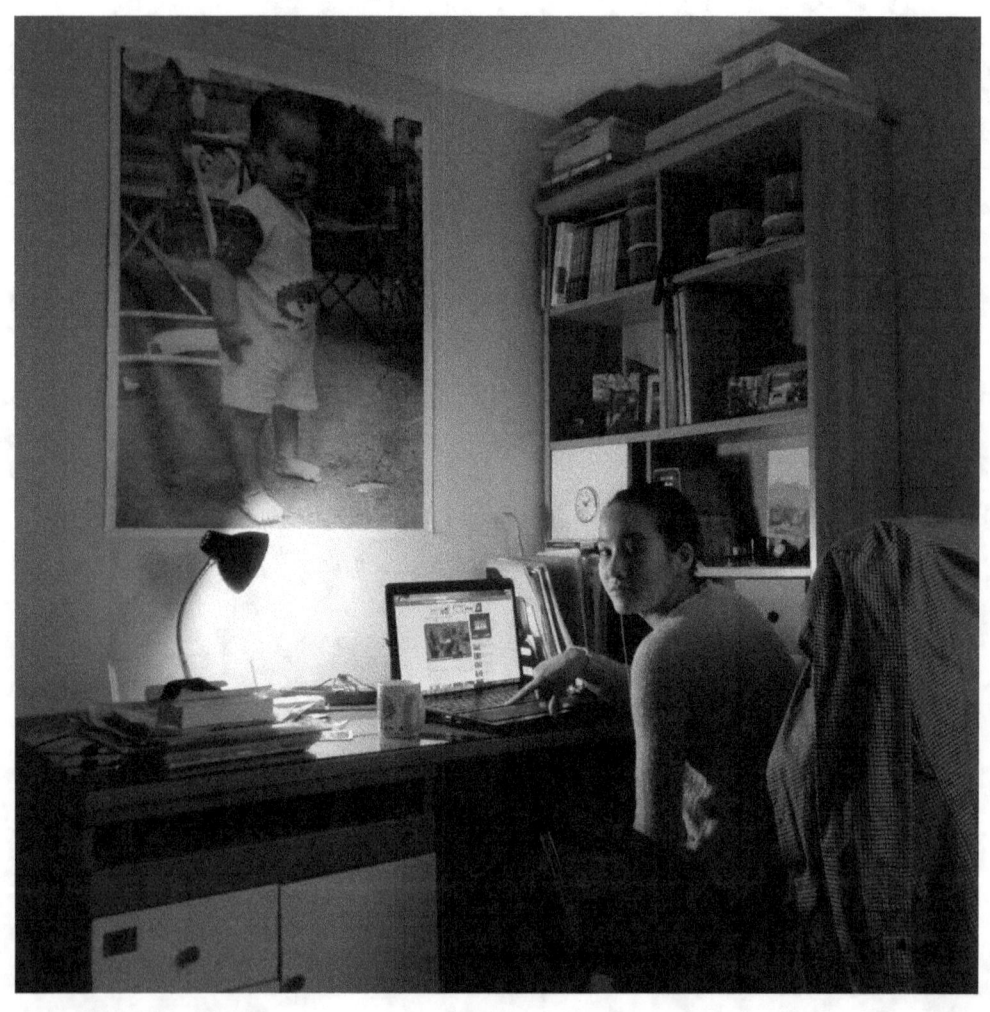

Everyone is Special

It's impossible to say anyone is just "fine."
But then again:
"Maya, how was ballet rehearsal today?" " Fine."
"Noa, how was the game today?" "Fine."
How are you feeling?" "Fine."
"How was the test?" "Fine."
We say "fine" an awful lot.
We are all becoming people who can't be bothered.

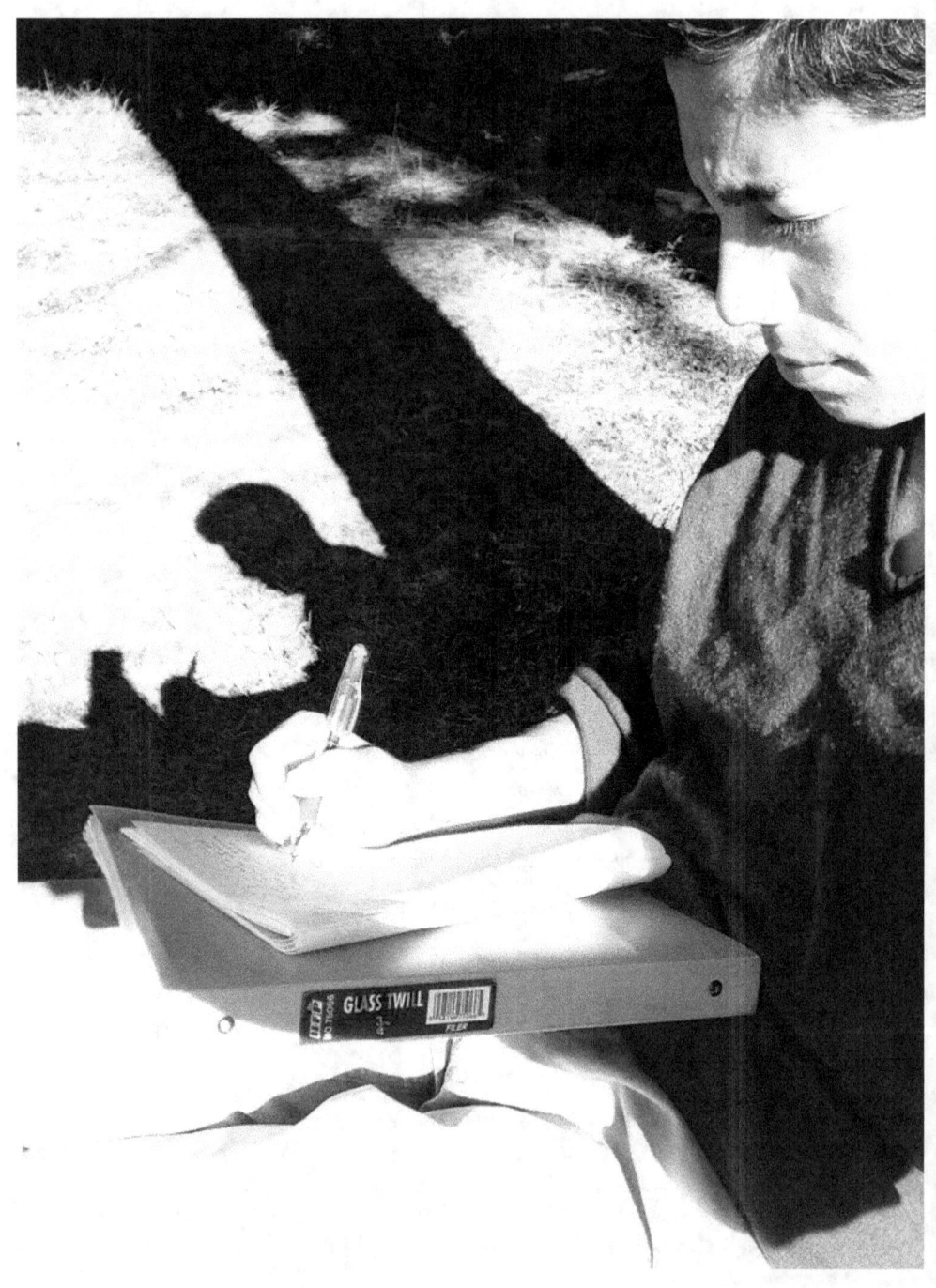

Is Life But a Walking Shadow?

I'm in a Shakespearean mood
But I'm not sure I'm hitting the mark.

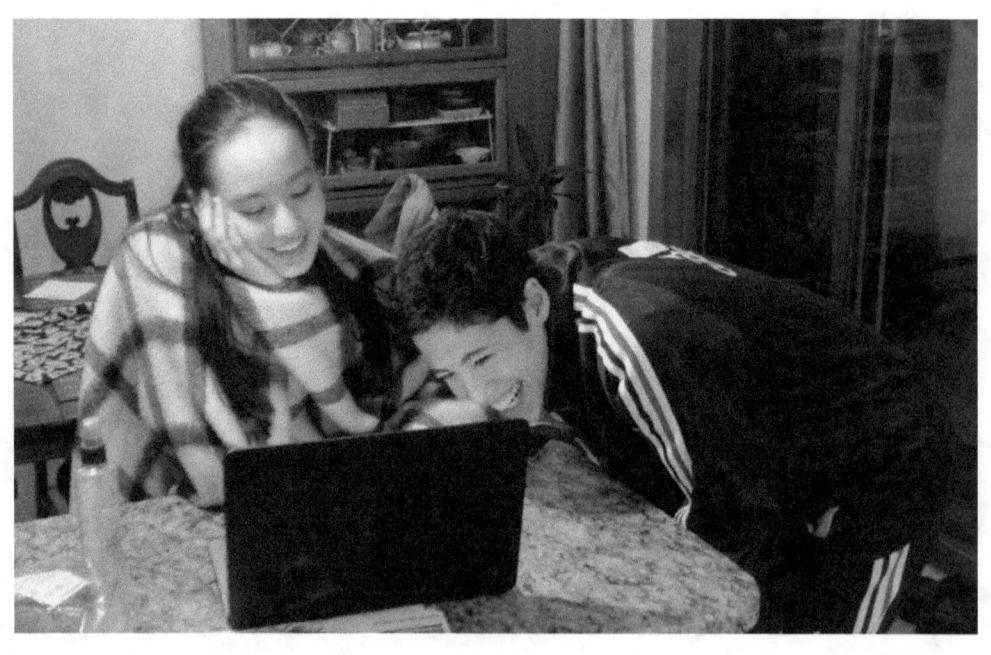

Time (or Space)

Time spreads out before us, seemingly still.
But even with time,
There is a quality, if you will,
A hardness, a difference in density.
Fun times are just such a thing.
The point is what we do with all this time that appears to stand still.
If we do nothing with it,
Time won't pass.
It will simply continue to spread out before us.

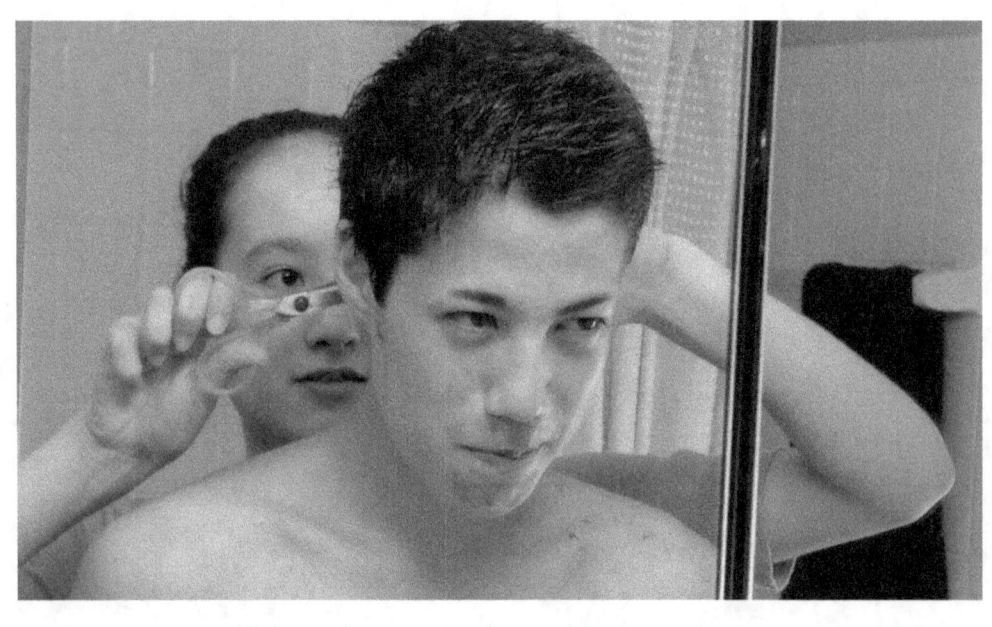

Handsome?
The baton has passed from Mom to Maya!

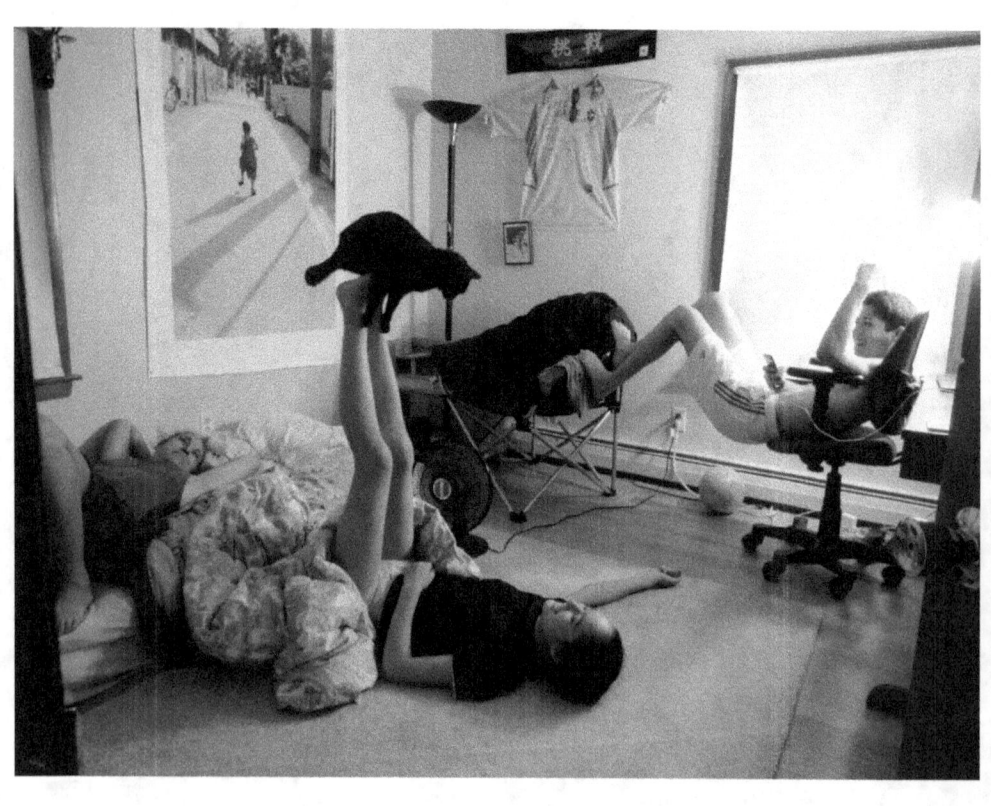

See You Again in Another 10 Years?
Kuropee too, together, of course.

But then...

2020 COVID-19 Pandemic!

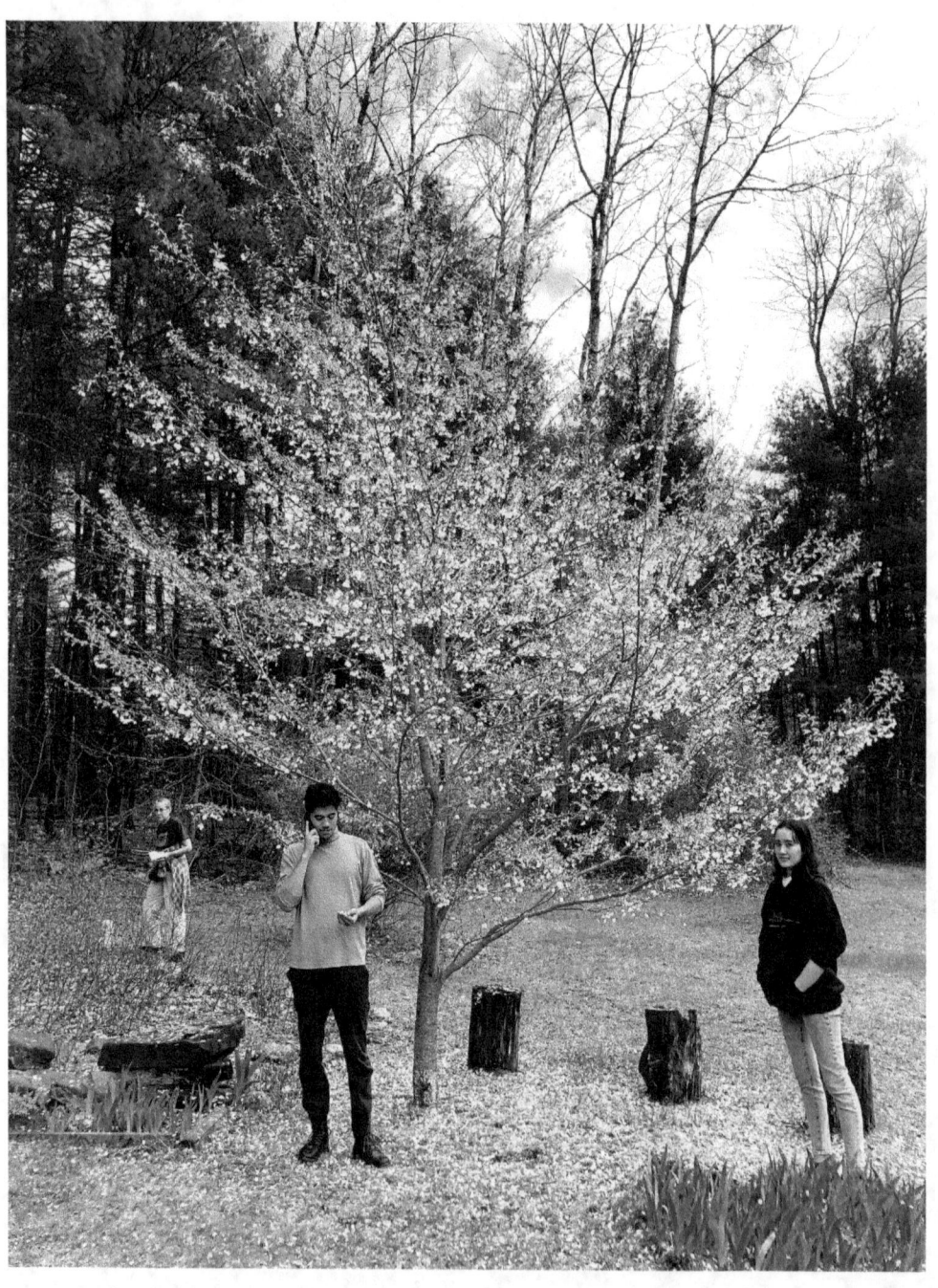

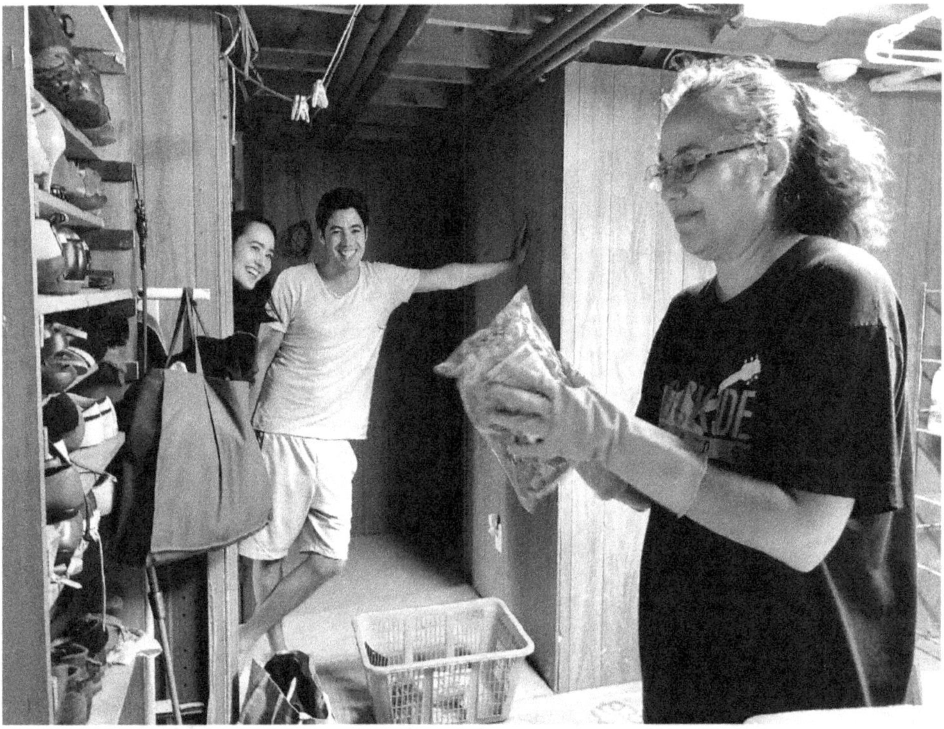

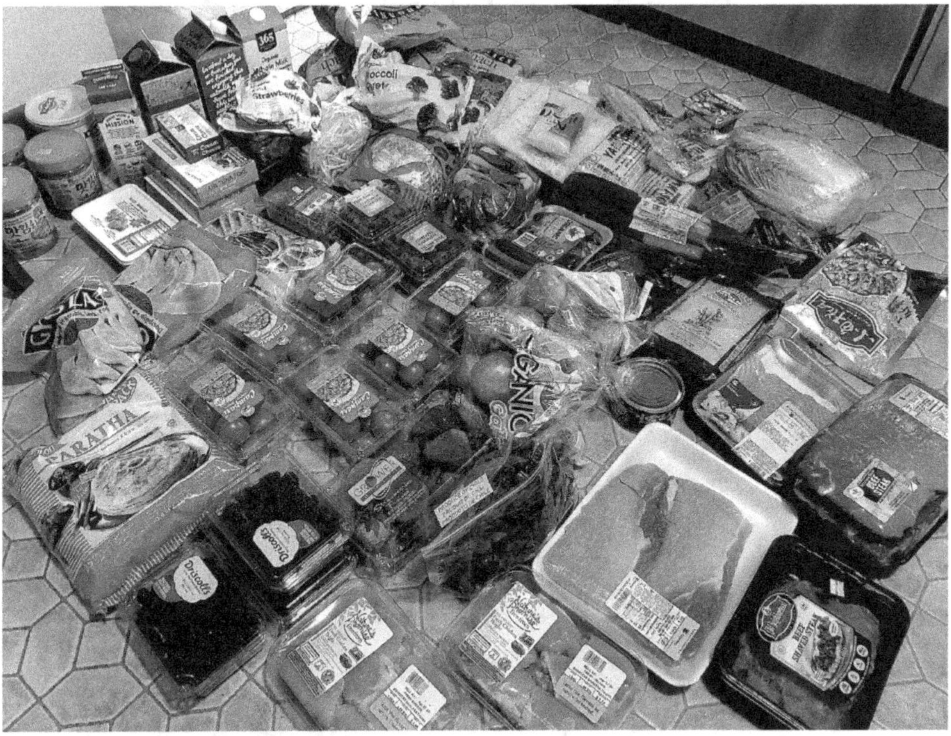

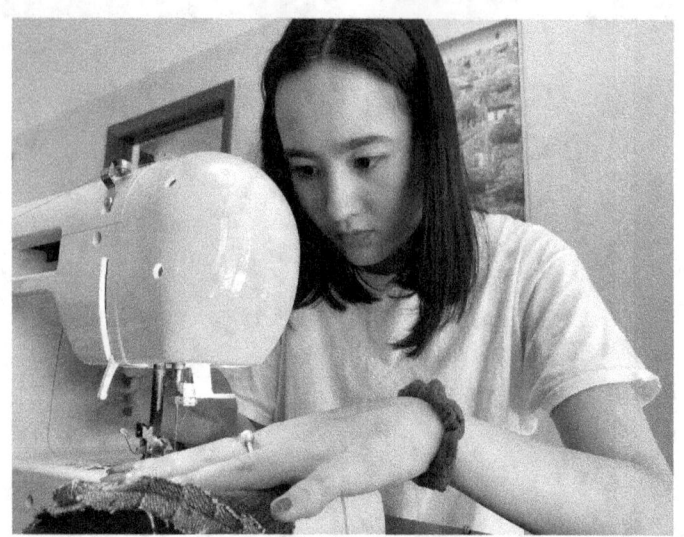
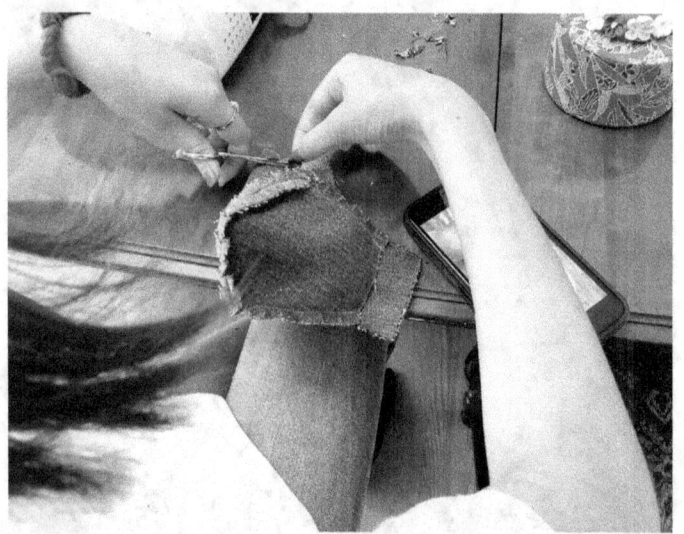
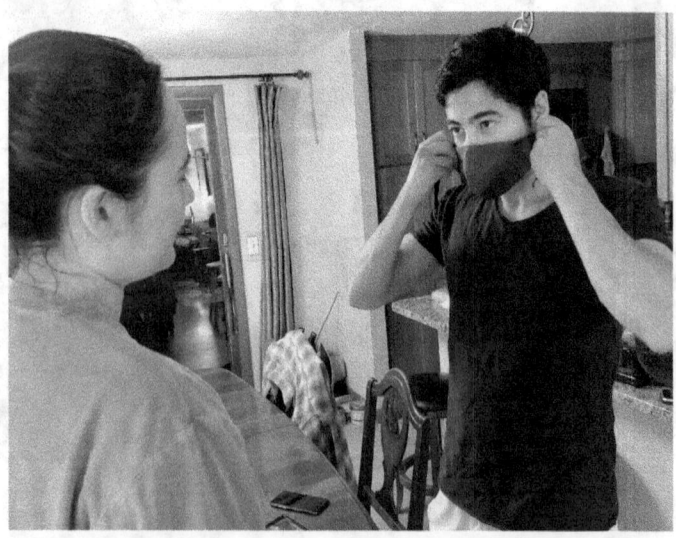

Face Masks, abruptly take center stage

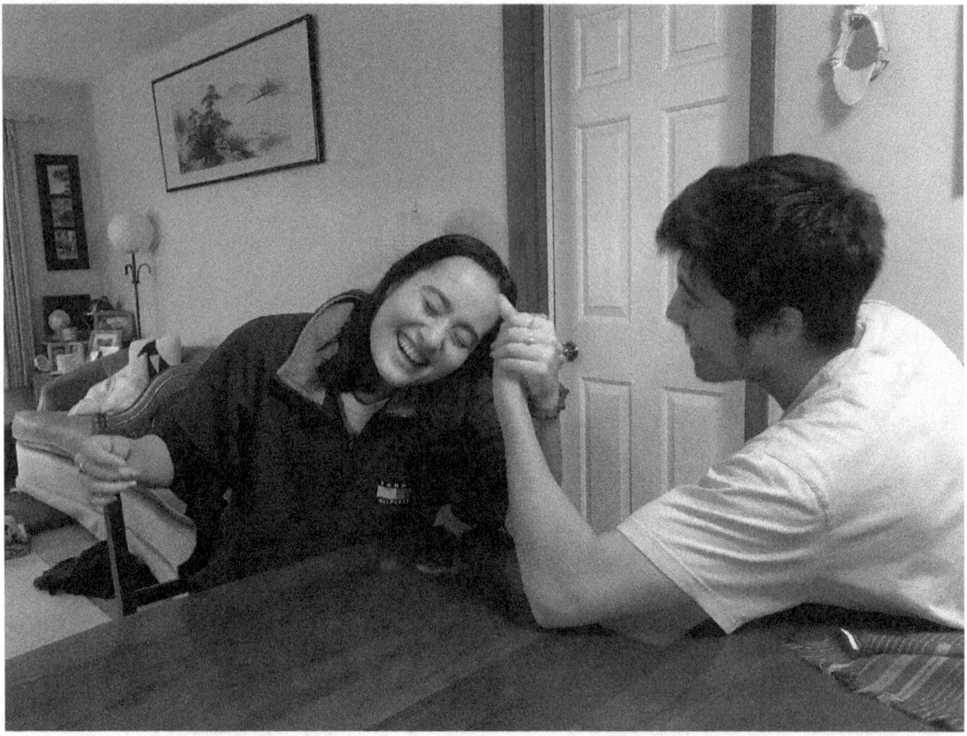

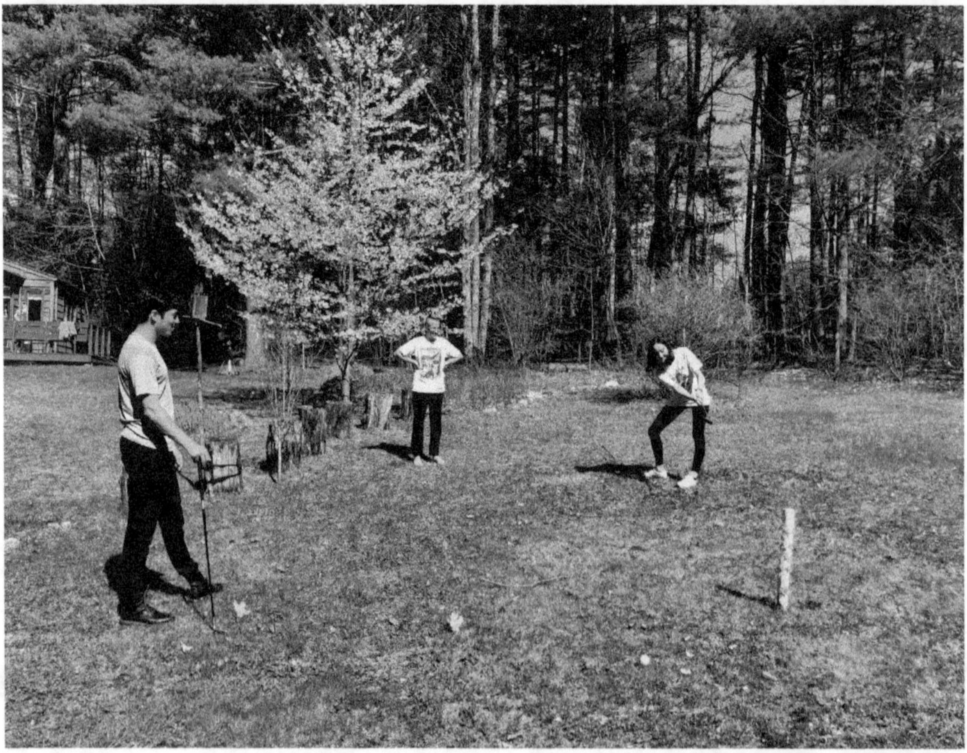

Stay home

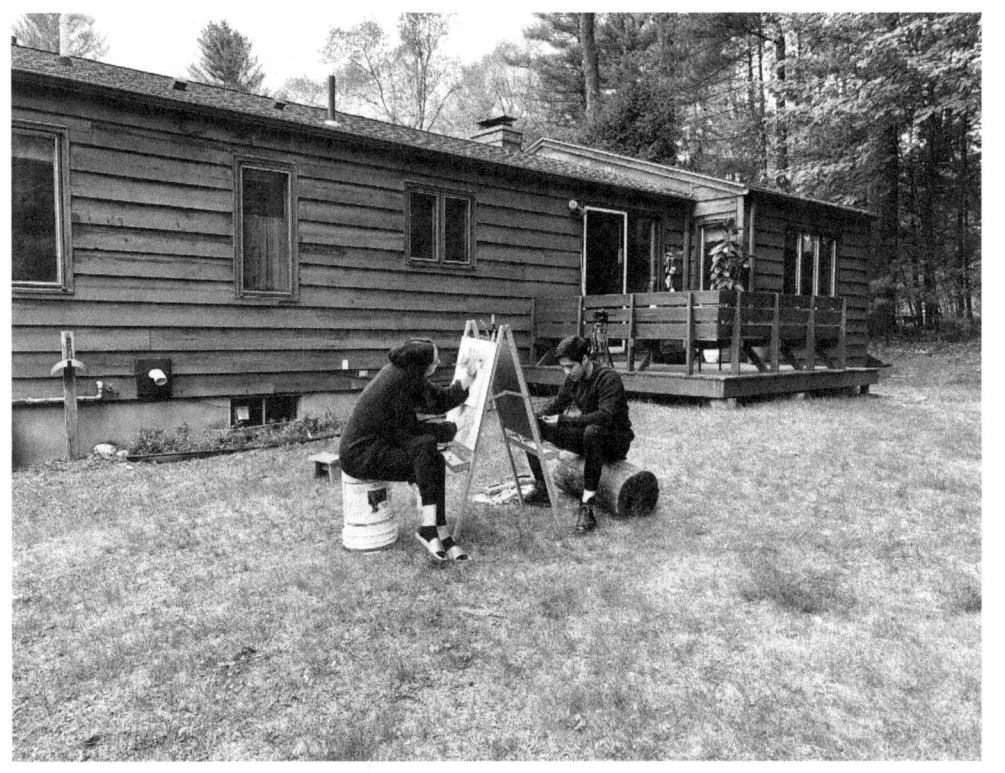

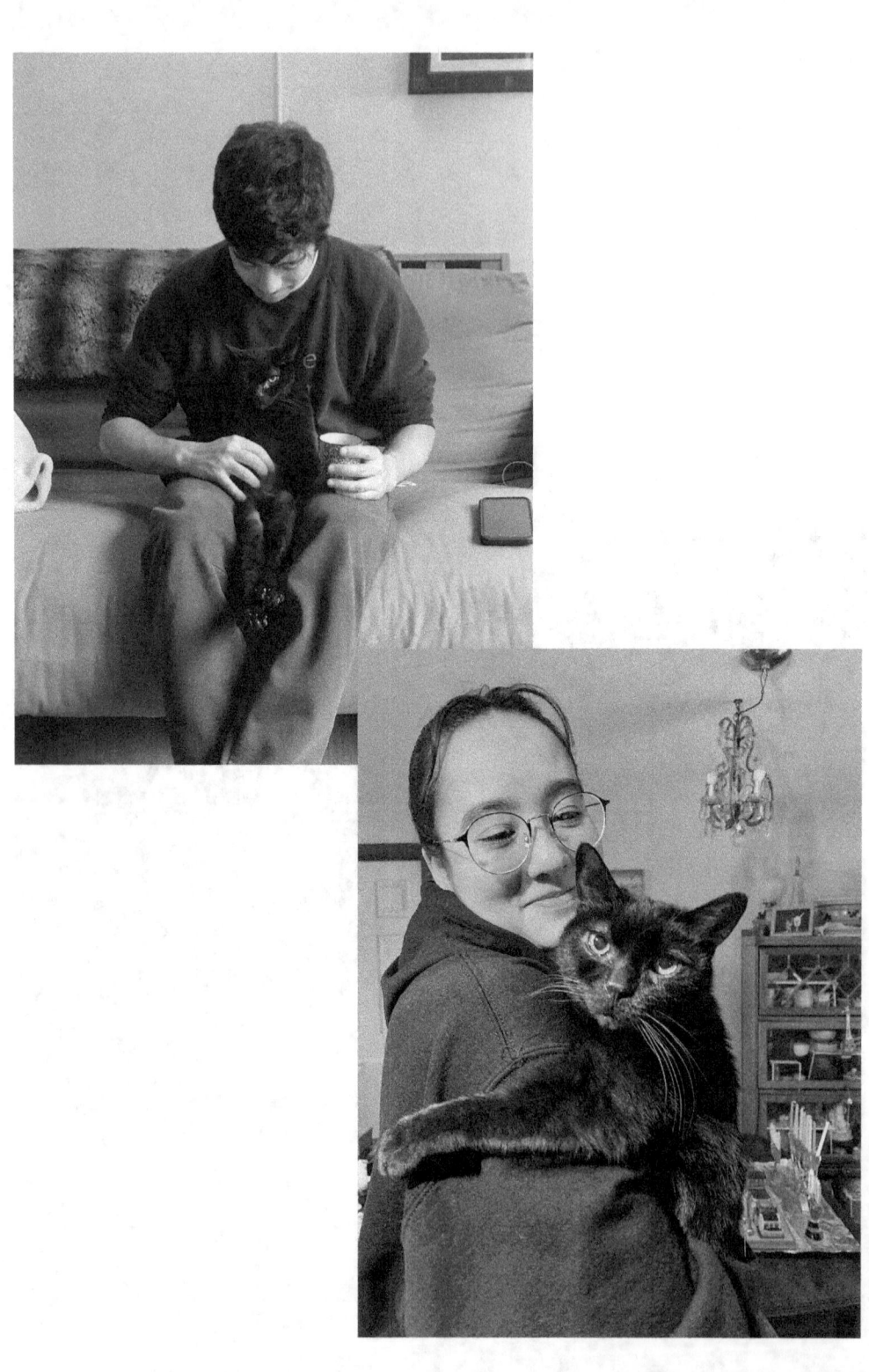

Kuropee, "as usual" as always

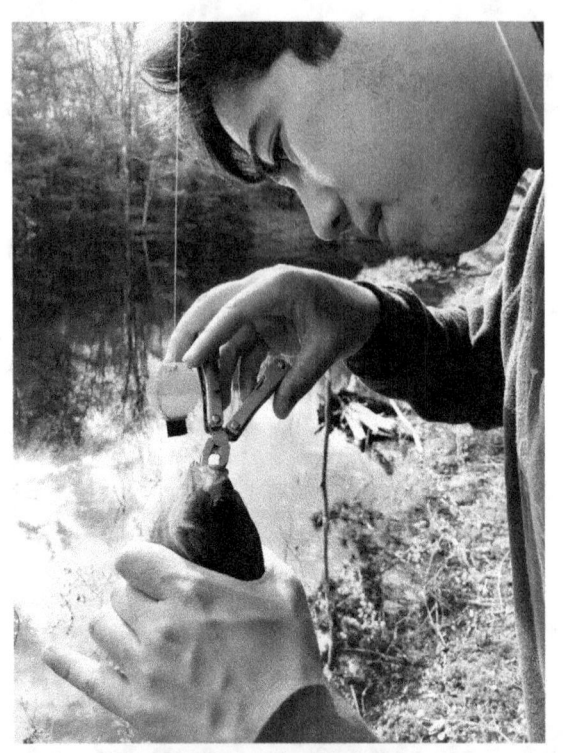

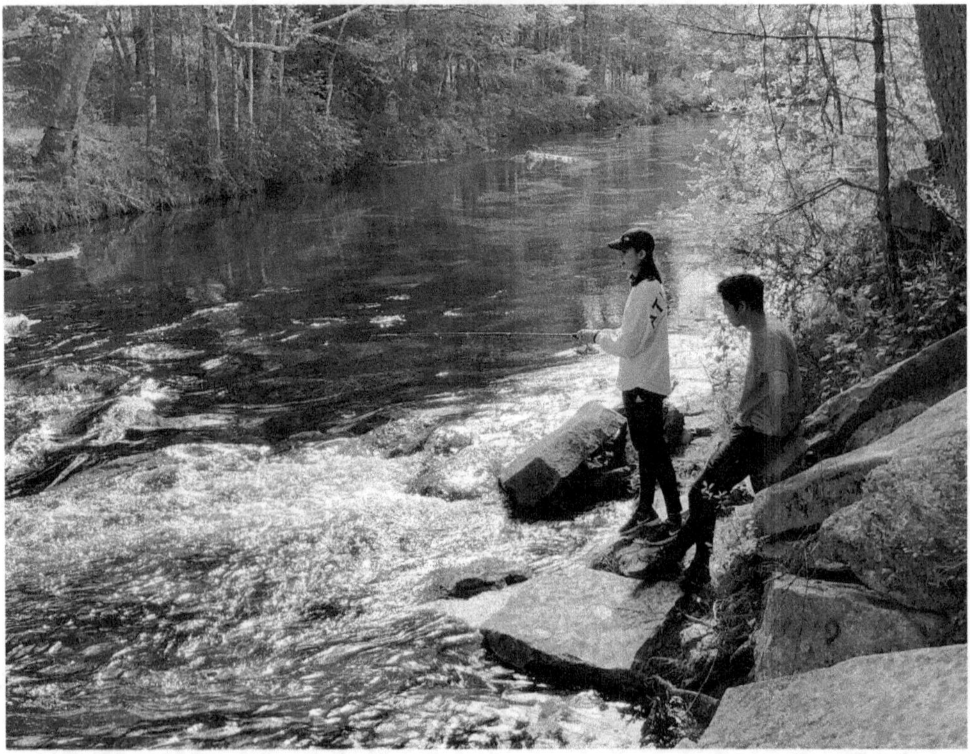

social distancing

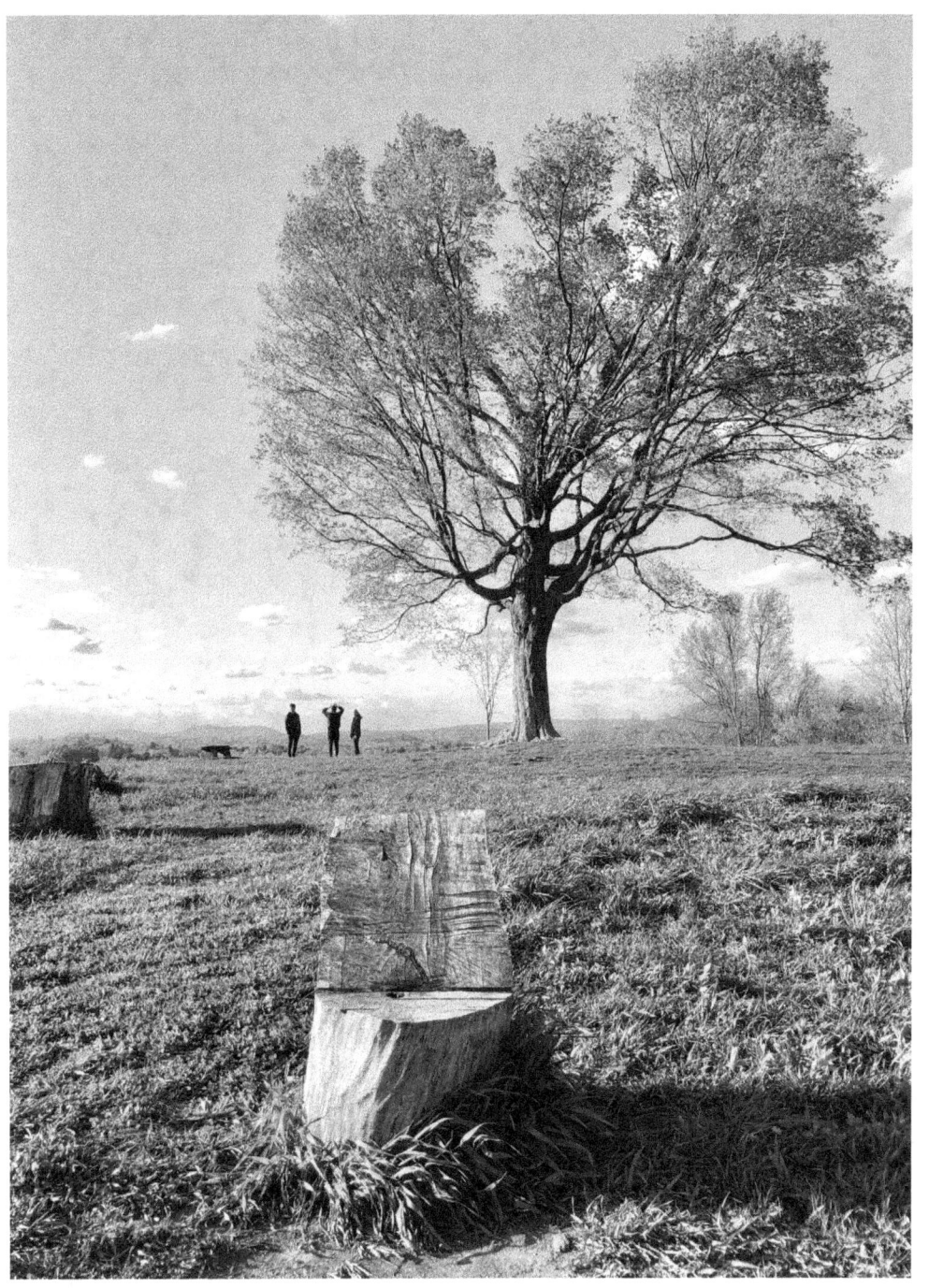

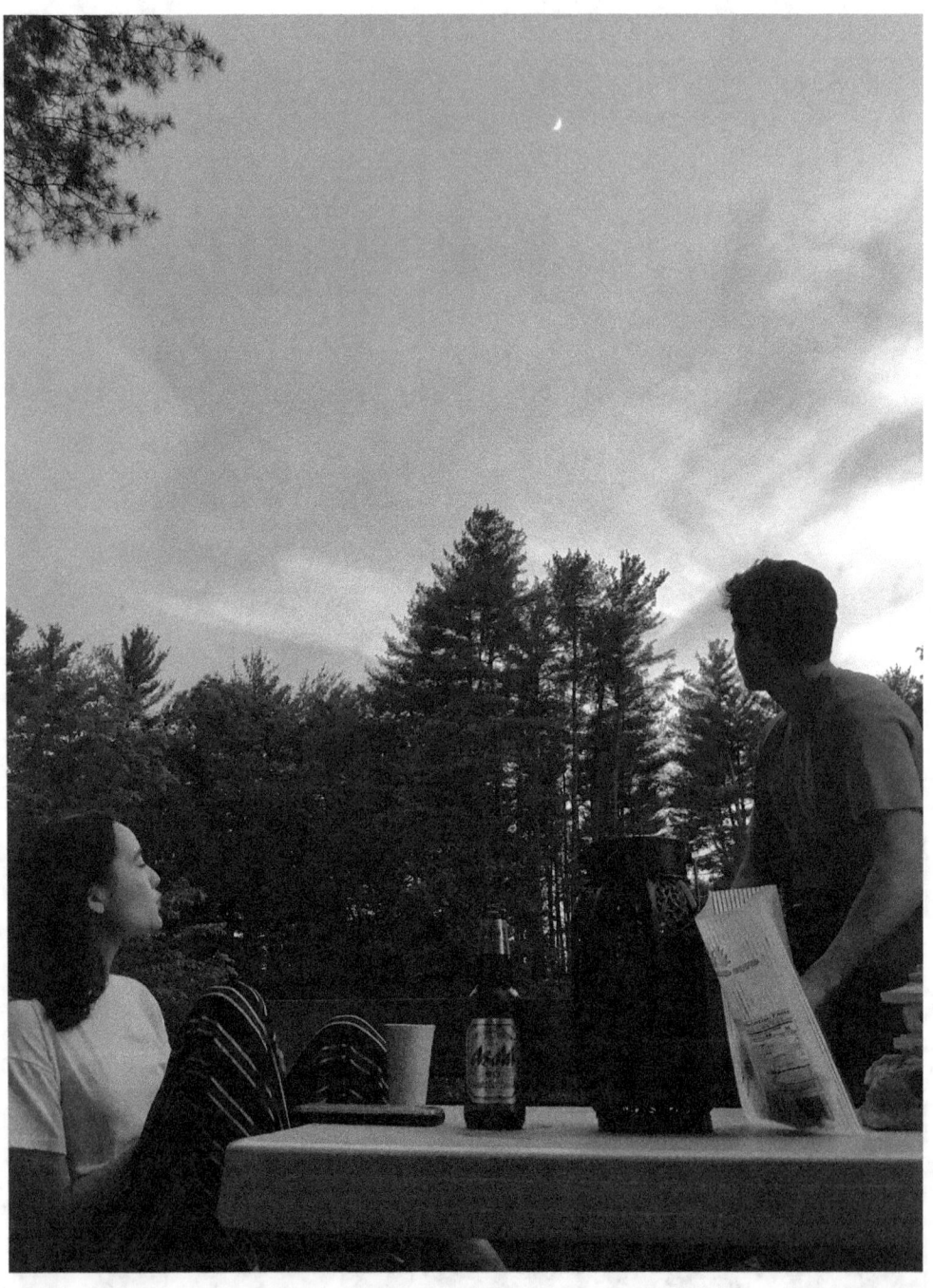

Wind of the Universe

Do you know the root of the word "corona"?
"Crown" in Latin
The ring of light enveloping the sun and celestial bodies You know?
That beautiful ring you see during a total solar eclipse
Currently on earth: the coronavirus pandemic
So, everyone
stay home
Social distance

Although earth remains earth···

What will happen now?
Will something change?
Social structure, demand for political fairness
For example:
Of course we do not need politicians who lie as if breathing
Then, do we change something?
Well···
At least I wish to become more kind, towards everything.

#BlackLivesMatter

Although earth remains earth···

"Lulala ride the wind of the universe!"
I like this phrase
"Robinson" a song by Spitz
Although it's from a little while ago

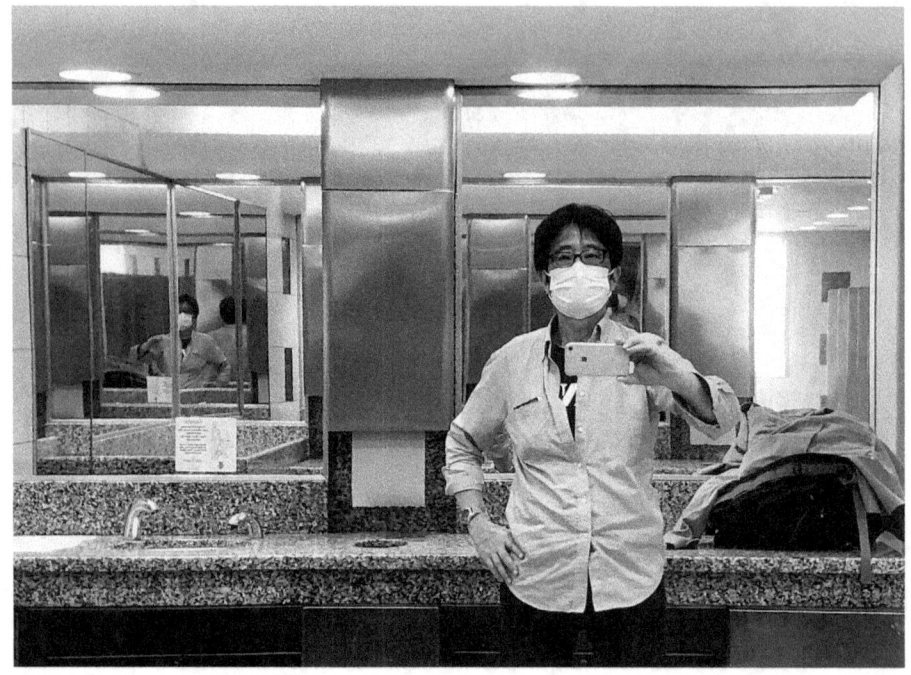

April 2020

Kazuhiko Iimura

Author Bio:
TV Director/journalist. Born in 1960. Director of multiple investigative TV news programs, most notably TV Asahi's program "The Scoop." Recent segments include "9-11:The Lies Bush Told" and "The Structure of Fabrication: 42 Years Late – The Truth Behind the Sayama Incident" among many others.
The original "Double" won third prize in the Visual Category of Shinpusha Publishing's 23rd competition in 2004. Previous publication: "NY is Laughing," published by Brain Publishing.

From the author

"Double" connects the past and the present for my wife and I. It is a memory-log of our children. It's underlying premise is the same for many people. The "I" from whose perspective it is written I am sure is just like the children of many other families; just like you were when you were a child. From this point in time, we cannot go back and increase the past. I have not recorded anything special here. It is our daily life which is so precious. It is so easy to forget. I wanted to indelibly imprint it on my soul. I looked through the viewfinder of the camera with that in mind, hearing Noa's voice threaded throughout.

I am certain of one thing.

If everyone were to try to remember how they were as a baby, even if only through photographs, then their true selves would be revealed and parents wouldn't abuse their children, children wouldn't stab their parents to death; tragic incidents would decrease dramatically. No one is born with an evil spirit.

Also, as the title suggests, my wife and I are strong proponents of referring to our children as "double" and not "half." When asked, "Is your child half?," we always answer, "They are double." They are not half of each, they are the whole of both.

It's as if you are saying to a child, "Are you only half human?"

No one would ever say that. I think that's an easy way to understand the issue.

Kazuhiko Iimura

{The above refers to the word "half" as used in Japanese when talking about biracial/bicultural children. The question asked is, "Is s/he 'half'?" To us and many others this carries the nuance of being "only half Japanese", not pure, and also without any appreciation of the other half as opposed to the way it might be phrased in English: " Is s/he half Japanese, half American?" The multi-cultural aspect is hardly ever addressed in Japanese.}

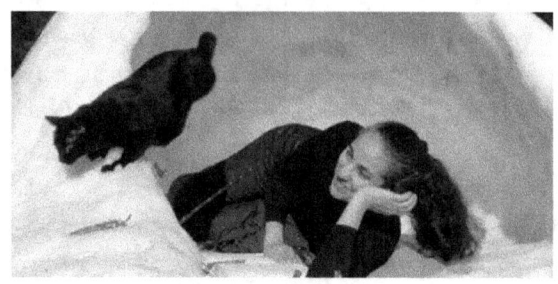

Brett Iimura

Translator Bio:
Has had a varied career including handsome cab driver in NYC, sign language interpreter, field producer for Japanese TV, childbirth educator and doula, all of which have required facility with multicultural and multilingual situations.

From the translator

In taking many of these photos I too, was hoping to set down memories for posterity, to enhance my own memory, and to give something to my children so they could look back and know more of their own childhood, where they came from, what they were like, our presence in their lives. If we know our roots we are more likely to know our true selves.

When I first saw Kazuhiko's manuscript along side the photos I saw it as a devotion to his children and found it difficult to translate. When I began to see it more as a love story the translation poured forth from the pages.

Each family has their own love story. Maybe Kazuhiko is right. If we all knew our own love story and how alike it is to everyone else's then maybe there wouldn't be so much hate in the world. We can only hope.

Brett Iimura

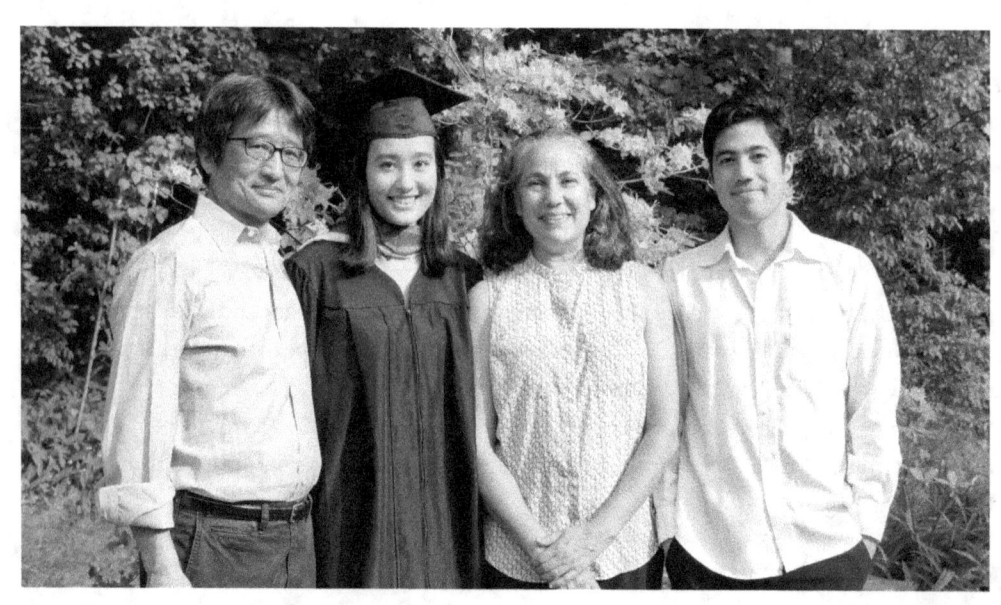

June 2020

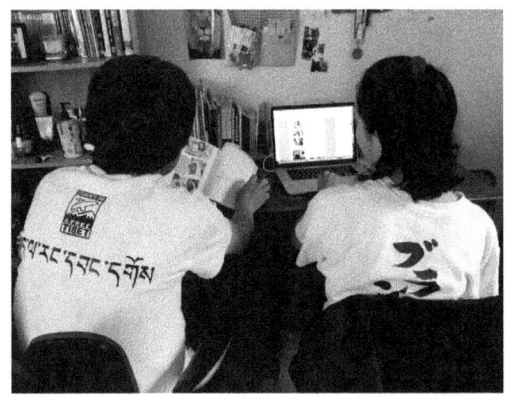

Published by Boundless Video productions
12 Thistle Lane
Amherst, Massachusetts, 01002 U.S.A
Copyright 2020 by Kazuhiko Iimura
Photo & Design : Kazuhiko Iimura
Photo & Translation: Brett Iimura
Photo: Noa Iimura
Translation & Layout: Maya Iimura
All rights reserved. This book may not be reproduced in whole or in part, without written permission from the publisher, except by a reviewer who may quote brief passages in a review; nor may any part of this book be reproduced, stored in a retrieval system, or transmitted in any form nor by any means including but not limited to electronic, mechanical, photocopying, recording, or other without written permission from the publisher.
June 2020

www.ingramcontent.com/pod-product-compliance
Lightning Source LLC
Chambersburg PA
CBHW071358210526
45465CB00001B/145